Beyond Self

Frontiers of Business Ethics

Series Editor
LASZLO ZSOLNAI
Business Ethics Center
Corvinus University of Budapest

VOLUME 12

PETER LANG
Oxford · Bern · Berlin · Bruxelles · Frankfurt am Main · New York · Wien

Beyond Self

Ethical and Spiritual Dimensions of Economics

by

LASZLO ZSOLNAI

PETER LANG

Oxford • Bern • Berlin • Bruxelles • Frankfurt am Main • New York • Wien

Bibliographic information published by Die Deutsche Nationalbibliothek
Die Deutsche Nationalbibliothek lists this publication in the Deutsche National-
bibliografie; detailed bibliographic data is available on the Internet at
http://dnb.d-nb.de.

A catalogue record for this book is available from the British Library.

Library of Congress Control Number: 2014933448

Cover design: Judit Kovacs, Createch Ltd, Hungary

ISSN 1661-4844
ISBN 978-3-0343-1772-6

© Peter Lang AG, International Academic Publishers, Bern 2014
Hochfeldstrasse 32, CH-3012 Bern, Switzerland
info@peterlang.com, www.peterlang.com, www.peterlang.net

This publication has been peer reviewed.

Printed in Germany

Contents

Foreword

We all look at the world through a personal pair of lenses – those we were born with, those that were culturally molded during our upbringing and education and later on refined via work, social environment, and family experiences, and those that are a result of mature reflection on what is important in one's life and in the life of others. Without such lenses that simultaneously focus and limit our perspectives we would not be capable of dealing with the enormous inputs from our senses and minds – and we would not be able to develop a sense of person, and with it a sense of what is good and just, on a personal as well as a collective level.

What has all this to do with a Foreword for the book you are about to read? It has to do with the reason why I am so pleased with this book and why I am so pleased with its author. And since the book's Introduction presents both its motivation and a concise overview of the contents, instead of commenting on the book, the following are a series of reflections on the book's author, my esteemed colleague and friend, Laszlo Zsolnai, and his many, varied, and significant contributions to the broad field that his lens and this book focus on.

I have had the privilege of knowing and sharing perspectives with Laszlo Zsolnai since we first met in 1997 in connection with the a meeting he organized for CEMS (originally the Community of European Management Schools, now Global Alliance in Management Education, based in Paris). At this meeting he fathered CEMS's Business Ethics Faculty Group; he is still its active chairman.

My contact with him was strengthened shortly thereafter when he invited me to contribute to the book he edited and published in 1998: *Business Ethics in the Community of European Management Schools*. In 2000 I attended the Central European University summer program that he led on Business and Ecology in Budapest. And in 2001, I participated in the first European conference on Spirituality in Management that he organized in Szeged, Hungary. Within this relatively short time span it became very clear to both of us that our 'lenses' were in synch. We not only shared perspectives on the need for expanding economics to include ethical and spiritual dimensions, the central themes in Laszlo's present book; we also appreciated and respected each other's person, integrity and search for meaning and fulfillment, that which is beyond words and numbers and analyses. In most of this interaction it was Laszlo who took the initiative.

I have never before encountered an academic who has used so much energy and talent to personally promote the thinking, writing and development of others who, more or less, share the world view that his lens creates and embraces. He has done this throughout his career and he continues to take initiatives, like an intellectual entrepreneur, motivating an ever wider circle of academics to focus their lenses on the ethical and spiritual dimensions of economics.

Like other well-known academics, he has published extensively – well over a hundred articles and book chapters as well as five books, all dealing with the major themes of the present book. Like other international academics, he is also an editor/ member of the editorial board of international journals. However, what distinguishes him from the rest of us is his focus on inspiring other intellectuals, directly or indirectly, both at home in Hungary and in the wide, wide world he inhabits, to contribute to the subversive goal of "undermining the self-interest doctrine" that he refers to in the Introduction to the book.

For example, in addition to being professor at Corvinus University of Budapest and Director of the Business Ethics Center there, he has been guest professor or visiting scholar at such renowned institutions as Cambridge and Oxford universities in the UK, University of California at Berkeley, University of Richmond and Georgetown University in the USA, University of St. Gallen in Switzerland, Heilbronn Business School in Germany, Bocconi University and the European University Institute in Italy, the International Institute for Applied Systems Analyses in Austria and Netherlands Institute for Advanced Study in the Netherlands. This impressive list is far from complete.

He has also been the organizer or co-organizer of significant international conferences in Europe, the USA and Asia that deal with these themes. One in particular comes to my mind, the conference on Spirituality in Management that he organized in Szeged, Hungary and which I briefly referred to earlier. At this workshop almost 12 years ago, and as best I know the first of its kind in Europe, he invited leading academics and a few business leaders to chart the progress of a spiritually-based perspective on leadership and to bring together people from around the world who could contribute to the future development of such a challenging and unorthodox paradigm in-the-making.

And finally I note that while most of us concentrate on writing and publishing our own articles and books, Laszlo has continually spent great time and energy in inviting others, both well-established and the lesser-known to focus on a theme within the broad framework of economics, ethics and spirituality, to write about the theme and then editing a book that presents the results. He has done this seventeen – yes seventeen times, as well as in series of books that he edits for major international publishing houses. I know of no other researcher in the broad fields he has covered who so selflessly has devoted so much time and energy to such a relatively thankless endeavor as editing the work of others.

Laszlo Zsolnai exemplifies the concept he introduces in the title of this book: "Beyond Self", which is the very essence of ethics and spirituality.

Peter Pruzan
Professor emeritus, dr.polit. & Ph.D.
Department of Management, Politics & Philosophy
Copenhagen Business School

Preface

This book addresses ethical and spiritual issues in economics. It contains previously published papers by the author. Only stylistic changes and updates have been made to the original versions.

The central idea advanced in the book is that the extreme focus on the self by economic actors leads to the destruction of both material and non-material values.

Amartya Sen describes the structure of self-interested behavior by focusing on three distinct features:

- self-centered welfare – one's welfare depends only on his or her own consumption;
- self-welfare goals – one's goal is to maximize his or her own welfare;
- self-goal choice – one's choice is guided by the pursuit of his or her own goal.

These assumptions represent the core of mainstream economics today. Throughout the book I argue that self-interest based actions and policies produce detrimental impacts on nature, future generations, and society at large.

If we want to survive and flourish in the material world we have to transcend the self and embrace wholeness. This value shift requires enormous changes in economics, politics, and social life but there seems to be no other option in view of today's state of ecological degradation and human suffering.

Once *Martin Heidegger* famously said, "Only a God can save us." I firmly believe that ethics and spirituality can do this job.

Laszlo Zsolnai

Acknowledgment

I am grateful to the co-authors of several papers published in this book. They include *Albert Bandura* (Stanford University), *Gian-Vittorio Caprara* (University of Rome "La Sapienza"), *Antonio Tencati* (Bocconi University, Milan), *Luk Bouckaert* (Catholic University of Leuven), *Hendrik Opdebeeck* (University of Antwerp), and *Knut J. Ims* (Norwegian School of Economics, Bergen). It was my pleasure and privilege to work with these excellent scholars and good friends over the last fifteen years.

I am also grateful to another old friend, *Peter Pruzan* (Copenhagen Business School) who kindly wrote the Foreword. I was greatly inpsired by *James March* (Stanford University), *Edwin M. Epstein* (University of California at Berkeley), and the late *Jozsef Kindler* (Corvinus University of Budapest) for transcending the self-interest culture of our age.

L. Zs.

PART 1

Introduction

CHAPTER 1

Economics, Ethics and Spirituality

World renowned organizational scholar, *James March* of Stanford University once said that *undermining* the *self-interest doctrine* may be the most important project of the 21st century (March 2011). The collected papers of this book aim to contribute to this enormous task.

Self-interest is at the heart of economics, politics and everyday life. People and organizations are encouraged to pursue their own self-interest without paying attention to the wider and longer term consequences of their choices and actions. The often celebrated 'Invisible Hand' doctrine states that individual self-interested behavior finally produces beneficial outcomes for all.

Self-interest maximization and free market competition are the basic pillars of the Invisible Hand doctrine which claims that self-interested competitive forces bring benefit for all. Overwhelming empirical evidence and strong theoretical arguments show that the working of the *Invisible Hand* is rather an exception than the general case.

There is a lot of controversy about the exact notion of the Invisible Hand doctrine. However, a commonly accepted understanding of the doctrine reads as follows: if individual actors follow their own self-interest in a competitive setting then this produces the optimal outcome for them collectively (Samuelson and Nordhaus 1989).

Conventional economic criticism lists some important factors which limit the beneficial effect of the invisible hand of the market. These factors include the existence of externalities, imperfect information and the undersupply of public goods (Stiglitz 2006).

There are important cases when self-interest based competition becomes destructive. One is the psychological case which shows that self-interested actors employ *moral disengagement mechanisms* which allow them to harm others both directly and indirectly. Another is the case of *positional arms race*, when competing actors want to improve their own relative position but arrive at a situation which is detrimental for them both individually and collectively. A third case is the *tragedy of the commons* when competing actors follow their narrow self-interest and destroy the collective good on which their survival depends.

Stanford psychologist *Albert Bandura* states that a division between thought and action takes place when people break the rules or get involved in dirty business. What is most surprising in rule violation and misconduct is that people are not bothered by their conscience, do not fear any sanction and do not feel obliged to make reparations (Bandura 1986).

The empirical findings by *Gian-Vittorio Caprara* and his team suggest that the more people are concerned with *self-enhancement goals*, the more they are inclined to resort to mechanisms that permit them to *disengage* from the duties and obligations of civic life and to justify transgressions when their self-interest is at stake. If economic agents become self-concerned then it is likely that – by employing moral disengagement mechanisms – their self-exonerative maneuvers will do *harm* to *others* (Caprara and Capanna 2006).

Based on behavioral evidence Cornell economist *Robert Frank* claims that the failure of the invisible hand is almost always inevitable as there is an inherent conflict between the interest of the individuals and the interest of the community as a whole (Frank 2011).

Frank shows that people care about relative wealth rather than absolute wealth. They are interested in social comparisons with their peers which in turn results in positional arms races for income, property and other objects of social status far beyond the optimal level of these positional goods.

The tragedy of the commons model developed by ecologist *Garrett Hardin* (1968) shows how self-interested individuals in free competition destroy their own common resources and ruin themselves. The model demonstrates the depletion of a shared resource by individuals, acting independently and rationally according to each one's self-interest, despite their understanding that depleting the common resource is contrary to the group's, as well as their own, long-term best interests.

In addition to the conventional solutions like governmental regulation and developing institutions for reducing destructive competition the papers collected in this volume suggest an alternative solution whereby the behavior of the competing actors can be enriched by *adopting explicit moral considerations*. Pro-social actors who consider the well-being of the community and measure success in broader terms than their own material welfare can avoid destructive competition. This solution is not far from the original insight of *Adam Smith* (1759) presented in his 'Theory of Moral Sentiments'.

The book's contributions

The paper *The Moral Economic Man* advances a view that economic behavior is multifaceted and context-dependent. This is in contrast to the so-called Homo Oeconomicus model which presumes that agents are perfectly rational, self-interest-maximizing beings. This model can be criticized on both empirical and normative grounds. The paper argues that understanding economic behavior requires a more complex and dynamic framework. The suggested departure point is the "I & We" paradigm developed by American sociologist *Amitai Etzioni* (1988) which states that economic behavior is co-determined by utility calculations and moral considerations. The paper emphasizes two major factors which can explain the ethicality of economic behavior; namely, the moral character of the agents and the relative cost of ethical behavior. It is argued that economic agents are moral beings, but the ethical fabric of the economy determines which face of the Moral Economic Man predominates.

The paper *Corporate Transgressions* is jointly written with *Albert Bandura* (Stanford University) and *Gian-Vittorio Caprara* (University of Rome 'La Sapienza'). It starts with the observation that corporate transgression is a well-known phenomenon in today's business world. Some corporations are involved in violations of law and moral rules that produce organizational practices and products that take a toll on the public. Social cognitive theory of moral agency developed by Bandura (1986) provides a conceptual framework for analyzing how otherwise pro-social managers adopt socially injurious corporate practices. This is achieved through selective disengagement of moral self-sanctions from transgressive conduct. The paper documents moral disengagement practices in famous cases of corporate transgressions and discusses some implications for business ethics on how to counteract organizational use of moral disengagement strategies.

The paper *Ethical Decision Making* states that the self-centeredness of modern organizations inevitably leads to environmental destruction and human deprivation. The principle of responsibility developed by German-American philosopher *Hans Jonas* (1984) requires caring for the beings affected by our decisions and actions. The paper argues that modern organizations should develop a critical sensitivity and empathy toward human and non-human beings with which they share a common environment. Ethical decision-making creates a synthesis of reverence for ethical norms, rationality in goal achievement, and respect for the stakeholders. The maximin rule is suggested to use in making decisions. It selects the "least worst alternative" in the multidimensional decision space of deontological, goal-achievement and stakeholder values. The ethical decision-maker is characterized as having the ability to take multiple perspectives and achieve an appropriate balance across diverse value dimensions.

The paper *Beyond Competitiveness: Creating Values for a Sustainable World* is jointly written with *Antonio Tencati* (Bocconi University Milan). It stresses that economics is rightly called a 'dismal science'. Mainstream economics propagates a negativistic view of human nature. In this view economic agents are always self-interested and want to maximize their own profit or utility. Their interactions are based on competition only and their sole criterion of success is growth measured in money terms. Mainstream economics generates vicious circles in which market players expect the worst from others and act accordingly. Competitive economics produces an enormous abundance of goods and services but at an intolerable environmental and social cost.

The paper argues that if we want to get closer to a sustainable world we need to generate virtuous circles in economic life where good dispositions, good behavior and good expectations reinforce each other. The collaborative enterprise model advanced in the paper promotes a view in which economic agents care about others and themselves and aim to create values for all the participants in their business ecosystems. Their criterion of success is mutually satisfying relationships with the stakeholders.

The paper *Management Needs Spirituality* emphasizes that the self-concept of decision-makers plays an important role in determining the ethicality of their decisions. Decisions can be understood as self-expressions of the decision-makers. The paper suggests that spiritual experiences have a vital function in developing the self of managers and improving the ethicality of their decisions. Spiritual intelligence can be understood as transformative intelligence that makes us ask basic questions of meaning, purpose, and values. It allows us to understand situations and systems deeply, to invent new categories, to be creative and to go beyond the given paradigms.

The conclusion of the paper is that spiritual intelligence is badly needed in management. Management decisions considerably affect the life and fate of human communities, natural ecosystems, and future generations. The well-being of these primordial stakeholders requires authentic care, which may develop from experiential one-ness with others and with the universal source of creation.

The paper *Future of Capitalism* argues that the moral foundation of capitalism should be reconsidered. Modern capitalism is disembedded from the social and cultural norms of society and has produced a deep financial, ecological and social crisis. Companies, regions, and national economies seek to improve their productivity and gain competitive advantage. Competitiveness usually produces monetary results at the expense of nature, society and future generations.

The paper suggests that the economic teachings of the world's major religions challenge the way capitalism is functioning, and that their corresponding perspectives are worthy of consideration. They represent life-serving modes of economizing which can assure the livelihood of human communities and the sustainability of natural ecosystems. The paper concludes that ethics and the future of capitalism are strongly connected. If we want to sustain capitalism we have to create a less violent, more caring form of it.

The paper on *Why Frugality?* is jointly written with *Luk Bouckaert* (Catholic University of Leuven) and *Hendrik Opdebeeck* (University of Antwerp). The paper defines frugality as an "art de vivre", which implies low material consumption and a simple lifestyle, enabling the mind to be receptive for spiritual goods such as inner freedom, social peace, justice or the quest for ultimate reality. Frugality signifies a release from egocentrism, opening the mind for the inner voice of conscience.

The paper argues that a genuine spirituality of frugality, leading to self-detachment and other-centeredness, does not exclude rationality. Spiritual-driven praxis of frugality needs rationally conceived plans. Frugal practices may lead to rational outcomes such as avoiding positional arms race in consumption and production alike. In this way economic actors may reduce ecological destruction, social disintegration and the exploitation of future generations.

The paper *Buddhist Economic Strategy* emphasizes that Buddhist economics is centered on want negation and purification of the human character. It challenges the basic principles of Western economics, (i) profit-maximization, (ii) cultivating desires, (iii) introducing markets, (iv) instrumental use of the world, and (v) self-interest based ethics. The paper reconstructs Buddhist economics and proposes alternative principles such as (I) minimize suffering, (II) simplify desires, (III) non-violence, (IV) genuine care, and (V) generosity. The paper argues that Buddhist economics is not a system but a strategy, which can be applied in any economic setting. Buddhist economics provides a rational, ethical, and ecological value background, which promotes happiness, peace and permanence.

The paper *Shallow Success and Deep Failure* is jointly written with *Knut J. Ims* (Norwegian School of Economics – Bergen) states that in our modern society, we tend to favor and celebrate short-term success, pseudo-solutions and window-dressing activities at the peril of ignoring long-term consequences. An obsessive hunt for short-term gains, often concretized as profit, produces detrimental effects for all life conditions. In the functioning of today's corporations, and in whole societies as well, we find many activities that result in grave failures rather than the creation of real solutions to pressing problems. The paper argues that we need scientific and technological knowledge, but we also need a better understanding of the existential conditions of human beings to avoid the fallacy of defining most problems as technical/economic/scientific and solving them in purely technical ways. We should gain a better understanding of self-realization and what this means in the perspective of deep ecology and sustainability.

The paper *Respect for Future Generations* starts with the observation that activities of present generations affect the fate of future generations for better or worse. What we do with our natural and cultural heritage mainly determines the way the members of future generations may live their own lives. Thus moral responsibility demands that we take into consideration the welfare of those who, without being consulted, will later be affected by what we are doing now.

The paper employs the principles developed by American legal scholar *Edith Brown Weiss* (1989) that underline our obligations to future generations: (1) Each generation should be required to conserve the diversity of the natural and cultural resource base. (2) Each generation should be required to maintain the quality of the planet. (3) Each generation should provide access to the legacy from past generations to future generations. The paper concludes that caring for future generations is not an altruistic concern only. Improving the position of future generations enhances the future of the present generations, too.

The paper *The Ethics of Systems Thinking* argues that in the case of a complex system we should consider all the important aspects of the system and create appropriate evaluation criteria for them. Systems theory suggests that the quality of life can be served by taking the view of whole systems. This requires considering all the relevant value dimensions, evaluating the performance of systems in adequate scales of measurement and using disqualification criteria for blocking trade-offs among non-substitutable values. The paper concludes that in our ecologically fragile, socially disintegrating world multidimensional decision making is a prerequisite for survival.

The paper *Redefining Economic Reason* stresses that the main goal of economic activities should not be profit-making but providing right livelihood for people. *Amartya Sen* (2004) suggests that economic reason can be understood as reasonableness of preferences, choices and actions. Reason requires that economic activities are achieved in ecological, future-respecting and pro-social ways. The paper argues that intrinsically motivated economic agents who balance their attention and concerns across diverse value-dimensions are able to do this. Organic agriculture, the Slow Food movement, ethical fashion, fair trade initiatives and ethical banking show the viability of true economic reason under the circumstances of present day 'rationally foolish' economic world.

In serving the survival of humankind we need agents who care about the natural environment and pursue self and community interests in a balanced way.

References

Bandura, A. (1986), *Social Foundations of Thought and Action: A Social Cognitive Theory*. Prentice Hall, Englewood Cliffs, NJ.

Brown Weiss, E. (1989), *In Fairness to Future Generations: International Law, Common Patrimony, and Intergeneration Equity*. The United Nations University, Tokyo & Transnational Publishers, Inc. Dobbs Ferry, New York.

Caprara, G-V. and Capanna, C. (2006), "Moral Disengagement in the Exercise of Civic-ness" Laszlo Zsolnai (ed): *Interdisciplinary Yearbook of Business Ethics*. Peter Lang, Oxford, pp. 85–96.

Etzioni, A. (1988), *The Moral Dimension*. The Free Press, New York.

Frank, R. (2011), *The Darwin Economy: Liberty, Competition, and the Common Good*. Princeton University Press, Princeton.

Hardin, G. (1968), "The tragedy of the commons" *Science* 162:1243–7.

Jonas, H. (1984), *The Imperative of Responsibility: In Search of an Ethics for the Technological Age*. Univ. of Chicago Press, Chicago.

March, J. (2011) *Private email communication with Laszlo Zsolnai* (February 26, 2011).

Samuelson, P. and Nordhaus, R. (1989), *Economics*. McGraw-Hill, New York & Singapore.

Sen, A. (2004), *Rationality and Freedom*. Harvard University Press, Cambridge MA.

Smith, A. (1759), *The Theory of Moral Sentiments*. A. Millar, London.

Stiglitz, J. (2006), *Making Globalization Work*. W.W. Norton, New York and London.

PART 2

Ethics in Business

CHAPTER 2

The Moral Economic Man*

Economic behavior is multifaceted and context-dependent. However, the so-called Homo Oeconomicus model states that agents are perfectly rational, self-interest-maximizing beings. This model can be criticized on both empirical and normative grounds. Understanding economic behavior requires a more complex and dynamic framework.

In the "I & We" paradigm developed by Amitai Etzioni, economic behavior is co-determined by utility calculations and moral considerations. Two major factors can explain the ethicality of economic behavior; namely, the moral character of the agents and the relative cost of ethical behavior.

Economic agents are moral beings, but the ethical fabric of the economy determines which face of the Moral Economic Man predominates.

1 Economic Behavior

It is a common belief in our age that people are motivated by their *own material well-being* when taking economic actions. This is the well-known Homo Oeconomicus image that depicts economic agents as rational, self-interest-maximizing beings. However, economic behavior is much more complex than the Homo Oeconomicus model suggests. People have rather

---

* First published: "The Moral Economic Man" in L. Zsolnai (Ed.) 2013: *Handbook of Business Ethics – Ethics in the New Economy*. Peter Lang, Oxford, Bern & Berlin, pp. 35–53.

different motivations, which may determine their economic choices (Jolls, Sunstein and Thaler 2000, Bowles and Gintis 2011).

Overwhelming empirical evidences suggest that

(i)   people care about their own material payoffs;
(ii) people consider the interest of others they know well;
(iii) people are willing to sacrifice their own material well-being to help those who are kind to them and to punish those unkind to them;
(iv) people take into account the well-being of strangers whose interests are at stake;
(v)   people are interested in their reputations – what others think about their behavior;
(vi) people care about their self-conceptions – what kind of persons they wish to be (Sunstein 2000).

Some interesting experimental results illustrate the above-noted behavioral features (i),....,(vi). The following famous studies provide strong *counterevidences* for the Homo Oeconomicus model. They suggest that *people* are *moral beings* in their economic actions.

1.1 The Ultimatum Bargaining Game

The ultimatum bargaining game has two players, an allocator and a receiver. The allocator is given $10 to distribute between the receiver and herself or himself. The receiver has two options: accepting the offer, in which case each player gets the amount proposed by the allocator; or rejecting the offer, in which case each player gets nothing. The players play the game only once.

The Homo Oeconomicus model presupposes that the allocator will propose $9.99 for herself/himself and only $.01 to the other player, and that the receiver will accept this offer on the grounds that the utility of one penny is greater than zero. But this is not what happens in reality. Offers usually average between $3 and $4. Offers less than $2 are often rejected.

Frequently there is a 50–50 division. These results cut across diverse cultures and the level of stakes (Sunsteins 2000).

1.2 Choices in Prisoner's Dilemma Situations

The Homo Oeconomicus model predicts that people will always defect in a prisoner's dilemma game situation. Each player may believe that it would pay more if she or he were non-cooperative since the other player is also expected to be non-cooperative.

Robert H. Frank and his colleagues conducted their prisoner's dilemma experiment with real money several hundred times. The subjects met in groups of three. Each was told that she or he would play the game once only with each of the other two subjects. Confidentiality was maintained so that none of the players would learn how their partners had responded in any play of the game. The rate of *cooperation* ranged between 40% and 62% (Frank et al. 1993).

To refine their experiment Frank and his colleagues asked subjects whether they would cooperate or defect in a one-shot prisoner's dilemma game if they knew with certainty that their partner was going to cooperate. The answers for cooperation ranged between 42% and 66% (Frank et al. 1993).

1.3 Lost Letter Experiment

Anthony M. Yezer and his colleagues conducted the so-called 'lost-letter' experiment (Yezer et al. 1996). The letter was placed in an unsealed, stamped, plain white envelope, with a single name and address on the front and no return address. Inside were ten $1 bills along with a brief handwritten note indicating that the enclosed currency was for repayment of an informal loan.

Thirty-two letters were left in upper level economics classes; an equal number of letters were left in upper level classes in other disciplines such as psychology, political science, and history. The Homo Oeconomicus model predicts that people will not return the lost letters. Contrary to this expectation, 31%–56% of the letters were returned.

This experimental evidence indicates that people display *respect* for the *interests* of *strangers*. The returned envelopes also provided some qualitative evidence on student reactions to the lost letters. In two cases, students added messages indicating that they had made extraordinary efforts to locate the addressee, including checking the student directory, the telephone directory and the university registrar (Yezer et al. 1996).

1.4 Contribution to the Public Good

In their pioneering study, *Gerald Marwell* and *Ruth Ames* designed an experiment where subjects were given some initial endowment of money that they were to allocate between two accounts, the 'public' and the 'private'. Money deposited in the subject's private account was returned to the subject dollar-for-dollar at the end of the experiment. Money deposited in the public account was pooled, multiplied by a factor greater than unity, and finally distributed equally among all subjects (Marwell and Ames 1981).

The Homo Oeconomicus model anticipates a subject putting the entire endowment into the private account. From a social point of view the optimal behavior is to put the entire endowment into the public account. Marwell and Armes found that subjects contributed an average of 20%–49% of their initial endowment into the public account. Certainly subjects were "*concerned with fairness*" when making their decisions (Marwell and Ames 1981).

1.5 Trust

In a game of trust, *Edward Glaeser* and his collaborators paired-off players, some of whom knew each other in real life. The first player received $15, of which he or she could give any part to the second player, hidden from view. The amount transmitted was doubled by the researchers, and the second player then sent any part he wished of the new amount back to the first player. Here the trusting outcome is for the first player to send the full $15 to the second. Then, provided that the second player is worthy of the first's trust, both can walk away with $15. Nevertheless, the Homo Oeconomicus model predicts that the first player will keep the entire $15.

The first players *sent* an average of $12.41 to their partners, who *returned* an average of 45% of the doubled sum. The existence of a previous acquaintance affected behavior: both the amount initially sent, and the percentage returned by the second player, rose in proportion to the length of time the players had known each other (Glaeser et al. 2000).

2 Problems of Rationality

The *rational choice model* has been widely used in economics, political science and other social sciences as a basic model of human choice behavior. The model states that the agent should maximize her or his utility function to be considered rational.

Agents are considered rational if their preferences are transitive and complete and they choose what they most prefer among the available alternatives. The rational choice model does not presuppose anything about the preferences people have. They may have self-centered, altruistic or even sado-masochistic preferences. The rational choice model represents a *formal theory* that says nothing about what people prefer or should prefer. Hereafter this model is referred as the *weak form* of *rationality*.

In economics and also in political science we can find a much stronger version of rationality where the assumptions of self-interest and perfect knowledge are added to the weak form of rationality. Hence we get the already discussed *Homo Oeconomicus* model according to which individuals are rational, exclusively self-interested and have perfect knowledge about the consequences of their choices. The Homo Oeconomicus model does have *substantive assumptions* about what people want and the manner in which they want it. This model is hereafter referred to as the *strong form* of *rationality* (Zsolnai 2008).

2.1 Bounded Rationality

Herbert A. Simon was a relentless critic of the rational choice model. He states that the model has overly strong claims on human beings. Real people have poor cognitive capacity and the information available to them is rather limited in most cases.

Agents in the real world are not capable of maximizing their utility function. Instead of maximizing, they usually make *satisficing* decisions. They usually choose the first available alternative that is good enough for them in the sense that it satisfies their aspiration level. This is the main message of the *theory* of *bounded rationality* for which Simon received the Nobel Prize in Economics.

Simon writes, "Faced with a choice situation where it is impossible to optimize, or where the computational cost of doing so seems burdensome, the decision maker may look for a satisfactory, rather than an optimal alternative. Frequently, a course of action satisfying a number of constraints, even a sizeable number, is far easier to discover than a course of action maximizing some function." (Simon 1987: 244).

The question arises of how a decision maker may set the level of criteria that define 'satisfactory'. Simon writes:

> Psychology proposes the mechanism of aspiration levels: if it turns out to be very easy to find alternatives that meet the criteria, the standards are gradually raised; if the search continues for a long while without finding satisfactory alternatives, the standards are gradually lowered. Thus, by a kind of feedback mechanism, or 'tatonement', the decision maker converges toward a set of criteria that are attainable, but not without effort. The difference between the aspiration level mechanism and the optimization procedure is that the former calls for much simpler computations than the latter. (Simon 1987: 244)

During the last decades abundant empirical evidence has been produced by economists and psychologists that shows that bounded rationality is important in real world situations.

2.2 *Myopic and Deficient Choices*

Psychologist *Daniel Kahneman* criticizes the rational choice model on the basis of research findings, which indicate that people are *myopic* in their decisions, may lack skill in predicting their future tastes, and can be led to *erroneous choices* by fallible memory and incorrect evaluation of past experiences (Kahneman 2011).

Kahneman differentiates between experienced utility and predicted utility. The *experienced utility* of an outcome is the measure of the hedonic experience of that outcome. The *predicted utility* of an outcome is defined as the individual's beliefs about its experienced utility at some future time. Predicted utility is an *ex ante* variable, while experienced utility is an *ex post* variable in the decision-making process.

According to the rational choice model, decisions are made on the basis of predicted utility. If experienced utility greatly differs from predicted utility then this may lead to sub-rational, or even irrational choices.

The problem of predicted utility raises the question: "Do people know what they will like?" The answer is a definite "No." The accuracy of people's hedonic predictions is generally quite poor. Experimental studies suggest two conclusions: (i) people may have little ability to forecast changes in their hedonic responses to stimuli; and (ii) even in situations that permit accurate hedonic predictions, people may tend to make decisions about future consumption without due consideration of possible changes in their tastes (Kahneman 2011).

Discrepancies between *retrospective utility* and *real-time utility* should also be addressed. This leads to the question: "Do people know what they have liked?" The answer is again a definite "No." Psychological experiments show that retrospective evaluations should be viewed with greater distrust than introspective reports of current experience. The results of studies support the following two empirical generalizations (Kahneman 2011).

(1) *The Peak & End Rule.* Global evaluations are predicted with high accuracy by a weighted combination of the most extreme affect recorded during the episode and of the affect recorded during the terminal moments of the episode.

(2) *Duration Neglect.* The retrospective evaluation of overall or total pain (or pleasure) is not affected by the duration period.

Since individuals use their evaluative memories to guide them in their choices toward future outcomes, deceptive retrospective evaluations may lead to erroneous choices.

Kahneman identifies two major obstacles to the maximization of experienced utility required by the rational choice model. People lack skill in the task of predicting how their tastes might change. It is difficult to describe as rational agents who are prone to large errors in predicting what they will want or enjoy next week. Another obstacle is a tendency to use the affect associated with particular moments as a proxy for the utility of extended outcomes. Observations of memory biases are significant because the evaluation of the past determines what is learned from it. Errors in the lessons drawn from experience will inevitably be reflected in deficient choices for the future (Kahneman 2011).

2.3 Rational Fools

Nobel Laureate economist *Amartya Sen* concluded that if real people behaved in the way that is required of them by the rational choice model then they would act like 'rational fools'.

Sen criticizes both the weak and strong forms of rationality. He refers to the weak form as 'internal consistency of choice' and to the strong form as 'maximization of self-interest'. He states

> It is hard to believe that internal consistency of choice can itself be an adequate condition of rationality. If a person does exactly the opposite of what would help achieving what he or she would want to achieve, and does this with flawless internal consistency (always choosing exactly the opposite of what will enhance the occurrence of things he or she wants and values), the person can scarcely be seen as rational. (...) Rational choice must demand something at least about the correspondence between what one tries to achieve and how one goes about it. (Sen 1987: 13)

Sen uses the term '*correspondence rationality*' to describe the correspondence of choice with the aims and values of the agent. He states that this kind of correspondence must be a necessary condition of rationality, regardless of whether or not it is also the sufficient condition. Correspondence rationality might be supplemented by some requirements on the nature of the reflection regarding what the actor should want and value (Sen 1987: 13–14).

It might well be arguable that rational behavior must demand some consistency, but consistency itself can hardly be adequate to ensure the rationality of choice. Internal consistency is not a guarantee of a person's rationality.

Rationality as *self-interest maximization* has additional problems. Sen asks, "Why should it be uniquely rational to pursue one's own self-interest to the exclusion of everything else?" Sen argues that the self-interest view of rationality "involves inter alia a firm rejection of the 'ethics-based' view of motivation. Trying to do one's best to achieve what one would like to achieve can be a part of rationality, and this can include the promotion of non-self-interested goals which we may value and wish to aim at. To see any departure from self-interest maximization as evidence of irrationality must imply a rejection of the role of ethics in actual decision making." (Sen 1987: 15).

According to Sen, "universal selfishness as actuality may well be false, but universal selfishness as a requirement of rationality is patently absurd." (Sen 1987: 16).

Rationality can be interpreted broadly as the discipline of subjecting one's choice – of action as well as objectives, values and priorities – to reasoned scrutiny. In the light of this definition reasonable economic choices should not necessarily satisfy the criteria of internal consistency of choice or maximizing self-interest. Economic choices should be subjected to the demands of reason (Sen 2002).

2.4 The Strategic Role of Emotions

Behavioral economist *Robert Frank* developed a model that emphasizes the role of the emotions in making choices. Frank argues that *passions* often *serve our interest* very well because we face important problems that are simply unsolvable by rational action. "Emotions often predispose us to behave in ways that are contrary to our narrow interests, and being thus predisposed can be an advantage." (Frank 1988: 4–7).

Human behavior is directly guided by a complex psychological reward mechanism. Rational calculations are the input for the reward mechanism. "Feelings and emotions, apparently, are the proximate causes of most behavior. (...) The reward theory of behavior tells us that these sentiments can and do compete with feelings that spring from rational calculations about material payoffs." (Frank 1988: 51–53).

The *modular brain theory* supports Frank's ideas. According to the modular theory, the brain is organized into a host of separate modules. Each module has its own capacity for processing information and motivating behavior. Most of these brain modules do not 'speak'; they simply do not have language capability. Even more importantly, these non-language modules are *not* equally well connected to the central language module of the brain. Perhaps this is the cause of the seeming disparity between different methods of assessing motivation.

Modular brain theorists view the language module of the brain as the center of our rational consciousness, obsessed with rationalizing all that we feel and do. However, there is a great deal of information that enters the central nervous system that cannot be accessed by the language module. The modular brain theory suggests "that when economists talk about maximizing utility, they are really talking about the language module of the left hemisphere, however, it does not account for all of our behavior. (...) The rational utility-maximizing language module of the brain may simply be ill-equipped to deal with many of the most important problems we face." (Frank 1988: 205–211).

Frank's main conclusion is that persons directly motivated to pursue their self-interest are often doomed to fail for exactly that reason. Problems can often be solved by persons who have abandoned the quest for maximal material advantage. The emotions that lead people to behave in irrational ways can indirectly lead to greater material well-being (Frank 1988: 258–259).

2.5 Social Norms

After a decade-long preoccupation with the rational choice model, sociologist *Jon Elster* developed an alternative theory that he calls the *theory of social norms* (Elster 1989, 2007). Elster contrasts rational action with norm-guided behavior. Rational action is outcome-oriented. Rationality says: "If you want to achieve X, do Y." Elster defines social norms as devices that are not outcome-oriented. Social norms say "Do X" or "Do not do Y" or "If you do X then do Y" or "Do X if it would be good if everyone did X."

> Rationality is essentially conditional and future-oriented. Its imperatives are hypothetical; that is, conditional on the future outcomes one wants to realize. The imperatives expressed in social norms are either unconditional or, if conditional, not future-oriented. In the latter case norms make the action dependent on past events or (more rarely) on hypothetical outcomes. (Elster 1989: 98)

Not all norms are social. There are two requisite conditions for norms to be considered social. First, they must be shared by other people and second, partly sustained by their approval or disapproval.

> In addition to being supported by the attitudes of other people, norms are sustained by the feelings of embarrassment, anxiety, guilt and shame that a person suffers at the prospect of violating them, or at least at the prospect of being caught violating them. Social norms have a grip on the mind that is due to the strong emotions their violations can trigger. (...) A norm, in this perspective, is the propensity to feel shame and to anticipate sanctions by others at the thought of behaving in a certain, forbidden way. (Elster 1989: 99–100 and 105)

Elster argues for the reality and autonomy of social norms. By the reality of norms he means that norms have independent motivating power. Norms are not merely 'ex post' rationalization of self-interest. They serve as 'ex ante' sources of action. Autonomy of norms means their *irreducibility* to *optimization.* Norms are *partly shaped* by self-interest because people often adhere to the norms that favor them. However, norms are not fully reducible to self-interest. The unknown residual is a brute fact (Elster 1989: 125 and 150).

2.6 The Communitarian Challenge

Communitarian thinkers criticize the *liberal conception* of the *self* that is at the heart of the rational choice model.

Philosopher *Charles Taylor* has argued that the liberal conception of the self is basically an atomistic conception of the person and that of human agency focusing exclusively on will and freedom of choice. Taylor defends a relational, inter-subjective conception of the self that stresses the social, cultural, historical and linguistic constitution of personal identity. By rejecting the voluntaristic conception of human agency he has formulated a cognitive conception that emphasizes the role of critical reflection, self-interpretation, and rational evaluation (Taylor 1985).

Catholic philosopher *Alasdair MacIntyre* defends a teleological and contextualist view of human agency. According to him, moral conduct is characterized by the *exercise* of *virtues* that aims at realization of the good. No agent can properly locate, interpret, and evaluate her or his actions except by participating in a moral tradition or in a moral community (MacIntyre 1988).

2.7 Feminist Criticism

In feminist literature the rational choice theory, and especially the strong form of rationality, is often criticized for presupposing an androcentric, male-biased conception of the human person, the so-called *separative self* (Ferber and Nelson (eds) 1993, Nelson 2006).

In her book "Beyond Self-Interest" *Jane J. Mansbridge* offers an alternative theory of choice that is inspired by feminine values. She distinguishes three forms of motivation, namely *duty*, *self-interest*, and *love*. Starting with her own case she says,

> I have a duty to care for my child, and I am happy by his happiness, and I get a simple sensual pleasure from snuggling close to him as I read him a book. I have a principled commitment to work for women's liberation, and I empathize with women, and I find a way to use some of my work for women as background to a book that advances my academic career. Duty, love (or empathy), and self-interest are intermingled in my actions in a way I can rarely sort out. (Mansbridge 1990: 134)

Mansbridge favors the coincidence of duty and love with self-interest. She says that both forms of non-self-interested motives (empathic feelings and moral commitments) are embedded in a social context, which makes them susceptible to being undermined by self-interested behavior on the part of others. Arrangements are required that generate some self-interested return for non-self-interested behavior to create an "ecological niche" for sustaining such behavior. Arrangements that make the absence of self-interested behavior less costly in self-interested terms increase the degree to which individuals feel that they can afford to indulge their feelings of empathy and their moral commitments (Mansbridge 1990: 136–137).

Based on the criticisms reported above we can say that the rational choice model is *empirically misleading* and *normatively inadequate*. For understanding economic behavior, a more complex and dynamic framework is needed.

3 The "I & We" Paradigm

Amitai Etzioni developed a theory that he calls *socio-economics*. He introduced the so-called 'I & We' paradigm that "sees individuals as able to act rationally and on their own, advancing their self or 'I', but their ability to do so is deeply affected by how well they are anchored within a sound community and sustained by a firm moral and emotive personal underpinning – a community they perceive as theirs, as 'We'." (Etzioni 1988: x).

Etzioni presents a new model of decision making in which two irreducible sources of valuations play a role, namely *pleasure* and *morality*. "Individuals are, simultaneously, under the influence of two major sets of factors – their pleasure, and their moral duty (although both reflect socialization). (...) There are important differences in the extent each of these sets of factors is operative under different historical and societal conditions, and within different personalities under the same conditions." (Etzioni 1988: 63).

The relationship between pleasure and morality is that while both affect choice, they also affect one another. However, each factor is only partially shaped by the other; that is, each factor has a considerable measure of autonomy. This co-determination model is shown by *Figure 1*.

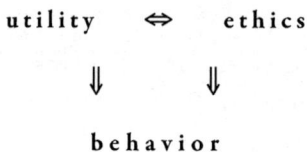

Figure 1 *Etzioni's co-determination model*

Etzioni states that "people do not seek to maximize their pleasure, but to balance their service of the two major purposes – to advance their well-being and to act morally." (Etzioni 1988: 83).

4 The Ethical Fabric of the Economy

Economic behavior is co-determined by utility calculations and moral considerations. The *major factors* that can help in understanding behavior can be identified:

(i)   the moral character of the agents;
(ii) the relative cost of ethical behavior.

Moral character refers to the strength of the moral beliefs and commitments of the agents. In a given situation the *relative cost* of *ethical behavior* is determined by the cost of an ethical option compared against the cost of the unethical option in terms of transaction cost and opportunity loss.

We can predict the ethicality of economic behavior by combining the moral character of the agents and the relative cost of ethical behavior. If the moral character of the agents is strong and the relative cost of ethical behavior is low, then ethical behavior can be expected. If the moral character of the agents is weak and the relative cost of ethical behavior is high, then unethical behavior can be expected (*Figure 2*).

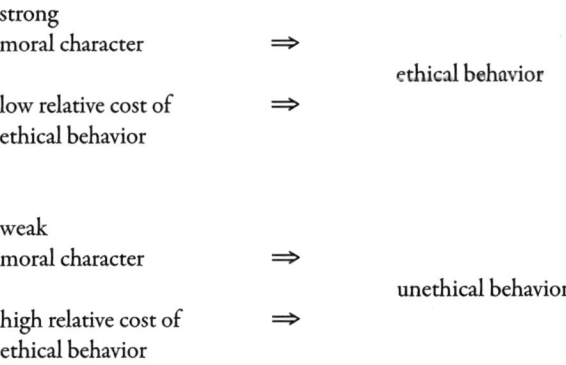

Figure 2 *Determinants of the Ethicality of Behavior*

The level of *corruption* in different countries is a good illustration. *Transparency International* produces the corruption ranking of countries year by year. Their ranking for 2011 is shown in *Table 1*.

Table 1 *Corruption Indices of Selected Countries in 2011*

Rank	Country	Score
1	New Zealand	9.5
2	Denmark	9.4
2	Finland	9.4
4	Sweden	9.3
5	Singapore	9.2
6	Norway	9.0
7	Netherlands	8.9
8	Australia	8.8
8	Switzerland	8.8
10	Canada	8.7
...		
24	United States	7.1
25	France	7.0
...		
50	Oman	4.8
50	Seychelles	4.8
54	Hungary	4.6
...		
177	Sudan	1.6
177	Turkmenistan	1.6
177	Uzbekistan	1.6
180	Afghanistan	1.5
180	Myanmar	1.5
182	Korea (North)	1.0
182	Somalia	1.0

Source: Transparency International 2011: Corruption Perceptions Index 2011.

A corruption index theoretically measures the likelihood that a particular economic transaction involves corruption in a given country. New Zealand, Denmark, Finland, Sweden, Singapore, and Norway are countries where corruption is virtually nonexistent. In these countries, economic agents have *high moral expectations* and at the same time, it is *easy* to *behave ethically*. In the most corrupt countries – such as Sudan, Turkmenistan, Uzbekistan, Afghanistan, Myanmar, North Korea and Somalia – economic agents have low moral expectations, and at the same time it is difficult to behave ethically.

5 Conclusions

Economic agents are moral beings. The context determines which face the Moral Economic Man predominates. Some hypotheses can be generated about the conditions, which mitigate the behavior of the Moral Economic Man for better or worse.

(i) The stronger the collective belief in the ethical norms by the economic actors, the more one can expect ethical behavior from them.

(ii) The stronger the pro-social orientation of the economic actors, the more one can expect ethical behavior from them.

(iii) The greater the social costs of transgression by the economic actors, the less one can expect unethical behavior from them.

(iv) The greater the transparency and accountability of the economic actors, the less one can expect unethical behavior from them.

Collective belief in the ethical norms, pro-socialness of agents, high cost of transgression as well as transparency and accountability are all preconditions for the proper functioning of the Moral Economic Man.

References

Bowles, S. and Gintis, H. (2011), *A Cooperative Species. Human Reciprocity and its Evolution*. Princeton University Press. Princeton and Oxford.

Elster, J. (1989), *The Cement of Society*. Cambridge University Press, Cambridge.

Elster, J. (2007), *Explaining Social Behavior. More Nuts and Bolts for the Social Sciences*. Cambridge University Press, Cambridge.

Etzioni, A. (1988), *The Moral Dimension*. The Free Press, New York.

Ferber, M.A. and Nelson, J.A. (Eds) (1993), *Beyond Economic Man*. The University of Chicago Press, Chicago & London.

Frank, R. (1988), *Passions Within Reason*. W.W. Norton, New York & London.

Frank, R.H., Gilovich, T. and Regan, D.T. (1993), "Does Studying Economics Inhibit Co-operation?" *Journal of Economic Perspectives* 1993 Spring, pp. 159–171.

Glaeser, E.L. et al (2000), "Measuring Trust" *Quarterly Journal of Economics* 115 (3): pp. 811–846.

Jolls, C., Sunstein, C.R. and Thaler, R.H. (2000), "Overview and Prospects" in Cass R. Sunstein (ed.): *Behavioral Law and Economics*. Cambridge University Press, Cambridge. pp. 13–58.

Kahneman, D. (2011), *Thinking, Fast and Slow*. Farrar, Straus and Giroux, New York.

MacIntyre, A. (1988), *Whose Justice? Which Rationality?* University of Notre Dame Press, Notre Dame IN.

Mansbridge, J.J. (1990), "On the Relation of Altruism and Self-Interest" in J.J. Mansbridge (ed.): *Beyond Self-Interest*. The University of Chicago Press, Chicago & London. pp. 133–143.

Marwell, G. & Ames, R. (1981), "Economists Free Ride, Does Anyone Else?" *Journal of Public Economics* 1981 June, pp. 295–310.

Nelson, J.A. (2006), *Economics for Humans*. The University of Chicago Press. Chicago and London.

Sen, A. (1987), *On Ethics and Economics*. Blackwell, Oxford.

Sen, A. (2002), *Rationality and Freedom*. Harvard University Press, Cambridge, MA.

Simon, H.A. (1982), *Models of Bounded Rationality*. The MIT Press, Cambridge & London.

Sunsteins, C.R. (2000), "Introduction" in Cass R. Sunstein (ed.): *Behavioral Law and Economics*. Cambridge University Press, Cambridge, MA. pp. 1–10.

Taylor, Ch. (1985), *Philosophical Papers*. Cambridge University Press. Cambridge, MA.

Thaler, R.H. (1991), *Quasi Rational Economics*. Russell Sage Foundation, New York.

Transparency International (2011), *Corruption Perceptions Index 2011*. Transparency International, Berlin.

Yezer, A.M., Goldfarb, R.S. & Poppen, P.J. (1996), "Does Studying Economics Discourage Co-operation? Watch What We Do, Not What We Say or How We Play" *Journal of Economic Perspectives* 1996 Winter, pp. 177–186.

Zsolnai, L. (2008), *Responsible Decision Making*. Transaction Publishers, New Brunswick and London.

Corporate Transgressions*

Corporate transgression is a well-known phenomenon in today's business world. Some corporations are involved in violations of law and moral rules that produce organizational practices and products that take a toll on the public.

Social cognitive theory of moral agency provides a conceptual framework for analyzing how otherwise pro-social managers adopt socially injurious corporate practices. This is achieved through selective disengagement of moral self-sanctions from transgressive conduct.

Moral disengagement practices can be recognized in cases of corporate transgressions. Business ethics is a major vehicle to counteract organizational use of moral disengagement strategies.

1 When Corporations Break the Rules

In the past decades corporate transgressions have became a major socio-political problem both in the developed and developing countries. The phenomenon of corporate deviance requires critical, cross-disciplinary studies that might illuminate the darker side of contemporary business practice. We have to acknowledge that one is dealing with institutional practices that are not easily examinable by conventional means. Study of

* First published: "Corporate Transgressions" in Laszlo Zsolnai (Ed.) (2002), *Ethics in the Economy – Handbook of Business Ethics*. Peter Lang, Oxford, Bern & Berlin. pp. 151–164. (Co-authors: *Albert Bandura and Gian-Vittorio Caprara*)

corporate transgressions is highly reliant on scandals, the media, public inquiries, police investigations, and whistle-blowers for glimpses of the concealed world of top management and its involvement in dirty tricks. Much research relies, then, on published secondary sources (Punch 1996).

Corporate transgression is about the exercise and abuse of power that is closely linked to the legitimate conduct of business. The essence of business is pursuit of legitimate interests of the parties involved in transactions circumscribed by rules that protect both the parties and their relationship to the interests of the public, society, the state, and regulatory agencies (Clarke 1990).

Although, a great deal of corporate transgression is never classified as crime, and the law plays a minor role in its regulation, the greatest discrepancy between common and white-collar violations is that corporations have the power to mobilize resources to influence the rules that cover their own conduct. In many cases, corporations actively defend their interests in ways that would normally be unthinkable for common law breakers (Punch 1996).

The most striking aspect of corporate transgression is that it is committed not by dangerous, criminally-oriented mavericks but by eminent members of the business community who break the rules ostensibly in the interests of their companies and their own interests (Levi 1987). The challenging question is why otherwise good managers engage in dirty business and why their conscience never bothers them (Punch 1996)? In this paper we draw on the theory and empirical findings of moral psychology to shed some light on this paradox.

2 Social Cognitive Theory of Moral Agency

Social cognitive theory addresses the exercise of moral agency (Bandura 1986, 1991). In this explanatory framework, personal factors in the form of moral thought and self-evaluative reactions, moral conduct and environmental influences operate as interacting determinants of each other. Within this reciprocal causation, moral agency is exercised through self-regulatory mechanisms. Transgressive conduct is regulated by two sets of sanctions, social and personal. Social sanctions are rooted in the fear of external punishment; self-sanctions operate through self-condemning reactions to one's misconduct. After people adopt moral standards, self-sanctions serve as the main guides and deterrents that keep behavior in line with moral standards.

The adoption of moral standards does not create a fixed control mechanism within the person. There are many psycho-social mechanisms by which moral control can be selectively disengaged from detrimental conduct (Bandura 1990, 1991). The mechanisms of moral disengagement enable otherwise considerate people to commit transgressive acts without experiencing personal distress.

2.1 Moral Justification

People do not ordinarily engage in reprehensible conduct until they have justified to themselves the rightness of their actions. In this process of moral justification, detrimental conduct is made personally and socially acceptable by portraying it in the service of valued social or moral purposes.

2.2 Euphemistic Labeling

Activities can take on markedly different appearances depending on what they are called. Euphemistic labeling provides a convenient tool for masking reprehensible activities or even conferring a respectable status upon them. Through sanitized and convoluted verbiage, destructive conduct is made benign and those who engage in it are relieved a sense of personal agency.

2.3 Advantageous Comparison

Behavior can also assume very different qualities depending on what it is contrasted with. By exploiting advantageous comparison injurious conduct can be rendered benign or made to appear to be little consequence. The more flagrant the contrasted activities, the more likely it is that one's own injurious conduct will appear trifling or even benevolent.

2.4 Displacement of Responsibility

Under displacement of responsibility people view their actions as springing from the social pressures or dictates of others rather than as something for which they are personally responsible. Because they are not the actual agents of their actions, they are spared self-censuring reactions. Hence, they are willing to behave in ways they normally repudiate if a legitimate authority accepts responsibility for the effects of their actions.

2.5 Diffusion of Responsibility

The exercise of moral control is also weakened when personal agency is obscured by diffusion of responsibility for detrimental conduct. Any harm done by a group can always be attributed largely to the behavior of others. People behave more cruelly under group responsibility than when they hold themselves personally accountable for their actions.

2.6 Disregarding or Distorting the Consequences

Additional ways of weakening self-deterring reactions operate by disregarding or distorting the consequences of action. When people pursue activities harmful to others for personal gain, or because of social inducements, they avoid facing the harm they cause or they minimize it. In addition to selective inattention and cognitive distortion of effects, the misrepresentation may involve active efforts to discredit evidence of the harm that is caused.

2.7 Dehumanization

Self-censure for injurious conduct can be disengaged or blunted by dehumanization that divests people of human qualities or attributes bestial qualities to them. Once dehumanized, they are no longer viewed as persons with feelings, hopes, and concerns but as subhuman objects.

2.8 Attribution of Blame

Blaming one's adversaries or compelling circumstances is still another expedient that can serve self-exonerate purposes. In moral disengagement by attribution of blame, people view themselves as faultless victims driven to injurious conduct by forcible provocation. By fixing the blame on others or on circumstances, not only are one's own injurious actions excusable but also one can even feel self-righteous in the process.

Moral disengagement can affect detrimental behavior both directly and indirectly. People have little reason to be troubled by guilt or to feel any need to make amends for harmful conduct if they reconstrue it as serving worthy purposes or if they disown personal agency for it. High moral disengagement is accompanied by low guilt, thus weakening anticipatory self-restraints against engagement in detrimental behavior. Self-exoneration for harmful conduct and self-protective dehumanization of others and treating them as blameworthy spawn a low pro-social orientation. Low pro-socialness, in turn, contributes to detrimental conduct in two ways. Having little sympathy for others both removes the restraining influence of empathetic considerateness of others and activates little anticipatory guilt over injurious conduct. Under some circumstances, effective moral disengagement creates a sense of social rectitude and self-righteousness that breeds ruminative hostility and retaliatory thoughts for perceived grievances.

3 The Personality of Corporations

A corporation is similar to personality in some important respects. First, the reciprocal causation operates among corporate modes of thinking, corporate behavior and the environment. Secondly, a corporation can be viewed both as a social construction and as an agentic system with the power to realize its intentions. Thirdly, corporate identity is crucial for the development and functioning of a corporation.

The practices of a corporation operate through self-regulatory mechanisms. These mechanisms regulate the allocation of resources in the pursuit of the goals and objectives of the corporation in accordance with its values and standards.

When corporations engage in reprehensible conduct they are likely to do so through selective disengagement of moral self-sanctions.

4 Moral Disengagement Strategies

The following brief analyses of famous business ethics cases illustrate the disengagement practices of corporation (*Box 1, 2, 3,* and *4*).

Box 1 *The Bhopal Case* (Weir 1987)

On December 3, 1984 the world's worst industrial disaster happened in Bhopal, India. Some 40 tons of methyl isocyanate (MIC) gas escaped from the Union Carbide pesticide production plant. At least 2,500 people were killed, 10,000 seriously injured, 20,000 partially disabled, and 180,000 others affected in one way or another.

Very early in the morning of that day a violent chemical reaction occurred in a large storage tank at the Union Carbide factory. A huge amount of MIC – a chemical so highly reactive that a trace contaminant can set off a chain reaction – escaped from the tank into the cool winter's night air. A yellow-white fog, an aerosol of uncertain chemical composition, speared over the sleeping city of 800, 000. The mist, which hung close to the ground, blanketed the slums of Bhopal. Hundreds of thousand of residents were rousted from their sleep coughing, vomiting and wheezing.

The Bhopal plant was operating by the Union Carbide India Ltd (UCIL), a subsidiary of the Union Carbide Corporation, headquartered in Danbury, Connecticut. Despite Indian law limiting foreign ownership of corporations to 40%, the US parent company was allowed to retain majority ownership (50.9%) of UCIL because it was considered a 'high technology' enterprise.

Union Carbide officials claimed that they did not apply a 'double standard' in safety regulation. Warren Anderson, the chairman of Union Carbide Corporation, insisted that there were no differences between the Bhopal plant and Union Carbide's West Virginia plant. This argument was erroneous but served as an advantageous comparison for Union Carbide. In reality, the Bhopal plant had violated the company's safety standards and operated in a way that would not have been tolerated in the United States.

Two years before the disaster a three-member safety team from Union Carbide headquarters visited the Bhopal plant, and submitted a revealing report on the safety dangers of the MIC section. The report recommended various changes to reduce the hazardous risks at the plant but the recommendations were never implemented. Union Carbide's main strategy was to displace responsibility by blaming the Indian government for its failure to effectively regulate the plant and for allowing people to live nearby.

Union Carbide was allowed to locate its factory in the middle of Bhopal, just two miles from the Bhopal railway station. It was convenient for shipping, but proved to be disastrous for the people living nearby. For years, the plant has been ringed with shantytowns, mostly populated by squatters. All three of the worst-affected communities in the disaster apparently existed before the Union Carbide plant opened. In court trials Union Carbide refused to pay anything to the Indian victims and their families, whose impoverished status made them easy to dehumanize and disregard.

Box 2 *The Ford Pinto Case* (Hoffman 1984)

On August 10, 1978, a tragic automobile accident occurred on US Highway 33 near Goshen, Indiana. Sisters Judy and Lynn Ulrich and their cousin Donna Ulrich were struck from the rear in their 1973 Ford Pinto by a van. The gas tank of the Pinto ruptured, the car burst into flames and the three teenagers were burned to death.

This was not the only case where the Ford Pinto caused serious accident by explosion. By conservative estimates Pinto crashes had caused at least 500 burn deaths. There were law suits against Ford because it had been proven that the top managers of the company were informed about the serious design problem of the model. Despite the warnings of their engineers, the Ford management decided to manufacture and sell the car with the dangerously defective design.

Ford used different moral disengagement strategies to defend its highly controversial decision. First, Ford continuously claimed that the "Pinto is safe," thus denying the risk of injurious consequences. Ford managers justified their claim by referring to the US safety regulation standards in effect until 1977. In doing so they displaced their responsibility for a car that caused hundreds of deaths to the driving practices of people, who would not have been seriously injured if their Ford Pinto had not been designed in a way that made it easily inflammable in a collision.

Ford engineers concluded that the safety problem of the Pinto could be solved by a minor technological adjustment. This would have cost only $11 per car to prevent the gas tank from rupturing so easily. Ford produced an intriguing and controversial cost-benefit analyses study to prove that this modification was not cost-effective to society. The study provided social justification for not making that option available to the customers.

Ford convinced itself that it is better to pay millions of dollars in Pinto jury trials and out-of-court settlements than to improve the safety of the model. By placing dollar values on human life and suffering Ford simply disregarded the consequences of its practice relating to safety of millions of customers.

Box 3 *The Nestle Case* (Post 1986)

Nestle has been the largest producer and seller of the infant formula products in Third World countries. Its marketing practice received world-wide criticism during the 1970s and 80s Infant formula is not harmful to the consumer when used properly under appropriate conditions. However, it is a demanding product that can be harmful to users when risk conditions are present. Nestle sold its infant formula to mothers in Africa, Latin America, and South Asia, many of whom lived under circumstances that made the use of such products a highly risky practice.

First, infant formula must be sold in powdered form in tropical environments, requiring that mothers mix the powder with locally available water. When water supplies are of poor quality, as they are in many developing countries, infants are exposed to disease. Second, since the product must be mixed, preparation instructions are important and mothers must be able to read it. However, the rate of female illiteracy is very high in many developing nations. Third, since infant formulas are relatively expensive to purchase there is a temptation to overdilute the powder with water. Unfortunately, overdiluted formula preparations provide very poor nutrition for infants. Having decided to bottle-feed their babies in order to increase their chances for a healthy life many mothers discovered to their horror that they had actually been infecting and starving their infants.

During the late 1970s the infant formula controversy became increasingly politicized in Europe and the United States. A Swiss public action group labeled Nestle as the "Baby Killer." Others claimed that Nestle causes 'commerciogenic malnutrition' in Third World countries – malnutrition brought about because of its commercial practices. In 1978 a powerful consumer boycott of Nestle and its products was begun in the United States. The company's representatives charged that the boycott was a conspiracy of religious organizations and an indirect attack on the free enterprise system. Nestle tried to defend and morally justify its questionable marketing practice by referring to the freedom of production and marketing. The Nestle statement was a political disaster. The company was denounced for its foolishness in the US media.

Companies may not close their eyes once their product is sold. They have a continuing responsibility to monitor the product's use, resale, and consumption to determine who is actually using the product and how they are using it. Post-marketing reviews are a necessary step in this process. In 1978 Nestle confessed that like other companies in the industry, they did no such research and did not know who actually used its products and the manner in which they did so. In this negligent attitude toward learning about the effects of its product, Nestle was acting on the strategy of disregarding the harmful consequences of its practice in developing countries. In 1984 Nestle's self-discrediting experience with the controversy over their infant formula finally came to an end by adopting the policy recommendations of WHO international marketing code. However, the company suffered a major blow to its reputation and to the morale of its employees. It is difficult to say how long it will take for Nestle to regain its good name and for the public to regard the company once again as a good corporate citizen.

Box 4 *The Three Mile Island Case* (Punch 1996)

The most severe accident in US commercial nuclear power plant history occurred at the Three Mile Island Unit 2 in Harrisburg on March 28, 1979. People were told to stay indoors and pregnant mothers and small children were advised to leave the area. There were widespread rumors of a general evacuation. Indeed, some 100,000 people simply voted with their feet and got up and left the area Although, there were no direct deaths or injuries, and there was talk of a possible explosion equivalent to a 1-megaton bomb. There were 4 million liters of contaminated water blown out of the system. Figures for the clean-up were initially set at somewhat between 200 and 500 million dollars. Ten years later the clean-up was still continuing.

Babcock and Wilcox built the reactor, the General Public Utilities ran Three Mile Island, and Metropolitan Edison owned it. During and after the event, Metropolitan Edison simple refused to face up to the seriousness of the situation. The company tried to distort consequences by continually issuing denials and minimizing the accident. In effect, the public was told there was no problem, no danger and all was following routine. They also used euphemisms and displacement of responsibility to 'operator error' in providing a public explanation that tended to play down the seriousness of the accident (Perrow, 1984).

Later on Metropolitan Edison made strong efforts to diffuse responsibility among the other main actors involved, namely Babcocks and Wilcox, General Public Utilities, and Nuclear Regulatory Commission. All endeavored to avoid blame for the accident in which the United States had just narrowly escaped its Chernobyl.

Table 1 shows the moral disengagement mechanisms used in the analyzed cases. The listed ones probably underestimate the scope of the mechanisms employed because they are confined to publicly observable manifestations of moral disengagement. The enlistment of exonerate practices is often buried in corporate memos and surreptitious sanctioning practices rather than publicly expressed.

Table 1 *Disengagement mechanisms used in different business ethics cases*

	Bhopal Case	Ford Pinto Case	Nestle Case	Three Mile Island Case
moral justification		+	+	
euphemistic labeling				+
advantageous comparison	+			
displacement of responsibility		+		
diffusion of responsibility				+
disregarding or distorting the consequences		+	+	+
dehumanization	+			
attribution of blame	+			

What is informative in the reported cases is that the moral collusion can end in justifying actions whose outcomes continue to be disapproved. The belief system of the corporation may remain unaffected for a long time by practices that are detrimental to it as well as to the general public. Selective disengagement mechanisms are deployed to mask such a contradiction and to perpetuate harmful corporate practices.

5 Conclusions

When the mechanisms of moral disengagement are at work in corporations, business ethics is difficult to manage, especially when the sanctioning practices are surreptitious and the responsibility for policies is diffused. Numerous exonerative strategies can be enlisted to disengage social and moral sanctions from detrimental practices with a low sense of personal accountability. A central issue is how to counteract moral disengagement strategies of corporations.

From the perspective of business ethics, there are several strategies for counteracting resort to moral disengagement. One approach is to *monitor* and *publicize* corporate practices that have detrimental human effects. The more visible the consequences on the affected parties for the decision makers, the less likely that they can be disregarded, distorted or minimized for long. Another approach is to *increase transparency* of the discourse by which the deliberation of corporate policies and practices are born. The more public the discourse about corporate decisions and policies, the less likely are corporate managers to justify the reprehensible conduct of their organizations.

Diffused and ambiguous responsibility structures make it easy to discount personal contribution to harmful effects. Instituting clear lines of *accountability* curtail moral disengagement. Exposing *sanitizing language* that masks reprehensible practices is still another corrective. The affected parties often lack social influence and status that make it easy to dehumanize and disregard them. They need to be *personalized* and their concerns publicized and addressed.

References

Bandura, A. (1986), *Social Foundations of Thought and Action: A Social Cognitive Theory*. Prentice Hall, Englewood Cliffs, NJ.

Bandura, A. (1990), "Mechanisms of Moral Disengagement" in W. Reich (Ed.): *Origins of Terrorism: Psychology, Ideologies, States of Mind*. Cambridge University Press, Cambridge. pp. 45–103.

Bandura, A. (1991), "Social Cognitive Theory of Moral Thought and Action" in W.M. Kurtines and J.L. Gewirtz (Eds): *Handbook of Moral Behavior and Development*. Lawrence Erlbaum Associates, Englewood Cliffs, NJ. Vol. 1. pp. 45–103.

Bandura, A., Caprara, G-V. and Zsolnai, L. (2000), "Corporate Transgressions through Moral Disengagement" *Journal of Human Values* 2000 (1), pp. 57–64.

Caprara, G-V. and Cervone, D. (2000), *Personality: Determinants, Dynamics, and Potentials*. Cambridge University Press, Cambridge.

Clarke, M. (1990), *Business Crime*. Polity Press, Cambridge.

Hoffman, M.W. (1984), "The Ford Pinto" in W.M. Hoffman and R.E. Frederick (Eds): *Business Ethics. Readings and Cases in Corporate Morality*. McGraw-Hill, Inc., New York. pp. 552–559.

Kurtines, W.M. and Gewirtz, J.L. (Eds): *Handbook of Moral Behavior and Development*. Lawrence Erlbaum Associates, Englewood Cliffs, NJ. Vol. 1–3.

Levi, M. (1987), *Regulating Fraud: White-collar Crime and the Criminal Process*. Tavistock, London.

Messick, D.M. and Tenbrunsel, A.E. (Eds) (1996), *Codes of Conduct: Behavioral Research Into Business Ethics*. Russell Sage Foundation, New York.

Perrow, C. (1984), *Normal Accidents*. Basic Books, New York.

Post, K.E. (1986), "The Ethics of Marketing: Nestle's Infant Formula" in W.M. Hoffman and R.E. Frederick (Eds): *Business Ethics. Readings and Cases in Corporate Morality*. McGraw-Hill, Inc., New York. pp. 416–421.

Punch, M. (1996), *Dirty Business. Exploring Corporate Misconduct*. Sage Publications, London, Thousand Oaks, New Delhi.

Weir, D. (1987), *The Bhopal Syndrome*. Sierra Club Books, San Francisco.

CHAPTER 4

Ethical Decision Making*

The self-centeredness of modern organizations leads to environmental destruction and human deprivation. The principle of responsibility developed by Hans Jonas requires caring for the beings affected by our decisions and actions. Ethical decision making creates a synthesis of reverence for ethical norms, rationality in goal achievement, and respect for the stakeholders. The maximin rule selects the 'least worst alternative' in the multidimensional decision space of deontological, goal-achievement and stakeholder values. The ethical decision maker can be characterized as having the ability to take multiple perspectives and make appropriate balances across diverse value dimensions. Modern organizations should develop a critical sensitivity to and empathy toward human and non-human beings with which they share a common environment.

1 Perverse Decisions of Modern Organizations

Modern organizations are *disembedded* from their environmental and social context and usually consider the natural environment and human persons as mere means to accomplish their own purposes and goals. The dominating *self-centered orientation* of modern organizations produces ecological destruction and human deprivation at large scale.

---

* First published: "Ethical Decision Making" in *Interdisciplinary Yearbook of Business Ethics*. 2006. Peter Lang, Oxford. pp. 99–119.

Perverse decisions of modern organizations appear in such phenomena as decision under risk and discounting in space and time. Prospect theory and the general theory of discounting can help us in describing and analyzing these phenomena.

1.1 Risky Decisions

The *prospect theory* developed by *Daniel Kahneman* and *Amos Tversky* is an empirically well-established theory that gives us a picture about the main regularities of decision making under risk (Kahneman and Tversky 1979).

Prospect theory states that decision makers display risk aversion in choices involving sure gains. For example, they prefer gaining $1,000 surely over gaining $10,000 with a 10 percent chance.

Prospect theory also states that decision makers display risk seeking in choices involving sure losses. For example, they prefer losing $10,000 with a 10 percent chance over losing $10,000 surely.

From prospect theory it follows that decision makers are more sensitive to losses than to gains. This means, for example, that they prefer gaining $1,000 surely and, at the same time, losing $10,000 with a 10 percent chance over losing $1,000 surely and, at the same time, gaining $10,000 with a 10 percent chance.

Risky decisions made by business and governmental decision makers often endanger the safety and integrity of the natural environment and human populations. The so-called *catastrophic risk* is a closely related phenomenon. The probability of catastrophes caused by modern, large-scale technologies is usually low but never zero. And the possible negative consequences are horrifying: irreversible destruction of ecosystems and enormous losses of human life.

The most tragic examples of this kind of ecological and human tragedy are the *Chernobyl* nuclear reactor explosion in 1986 that sent nuclear fallout across Europe, increasing human and animal cancers, and the wreck of the *Exxon Valdez* oil tanker at the Alaskan coastline in 1989 that produced the largest oil spill in American history.

1.2 Discounting in Space and Time

Decision makers usually overvalue things here and now in comparison with things far and later. This phenomenon is produced by the mechanism of *discounting*.

According to the general theory of discounting, decision makers discount gains that are distant in space and time. For example, they prefer gaining $1,000 here and now over gaining $1,000 far and later. "A bird in the hand is worth two in the bush."

According to the general theory of discounting, decision makers put off negative things till the morrow because they discount losses that are distant in space and time. For example, they would rather lose $1,000 far and later than here and now.

From the general theory of discounting it follows that decision makers undervalue both gains and losses that are distant in space and time. For example, they prefer gaining $1,000 here and now and losing $1,000 far and later over losing $1,000 here and now and gaining $1,000 far and later.

Decision makers use discount rates to value things distant in space and time. The *present value* of a thing is usually calculated as follows:

$$T = t / (1 + \alpha)^x$$

where T is the present value of the thing t, x is a measure of the distance of t in space or in time, and α is the discount rate, which is usually between 5 percent and 15 percent.

If the distance of a thing in space and/or time is great enough then its present value becomes extremely small. Also, the present value depends on the applied discount rate: the greater the discount rate, the smaller the present value. The present value of a thing is determined by the applied discount rate and its distance in space and time.

Discounting in space and time may produce negative consequences in business and governmental decision making. Decision makers, who strongly discount things in space and time, are interested in neither the solutions of long-range ecological and human problems, nor the global impacts of their activities on the natural environment and human communities.

The *international trade* in *hazardous wastes* is an illustrative case in point. American and West-European countries transport and dump hazardous wastes in distant and less-developed Third World countries, without displaying any interest in the future ecological and human health impacts of these materials (Sing and Lakhan 1989).

1.3 Self-Centered Organizations

By combining the main lessons of prospect theory and the general theory of discounting we can arrive at a better understanding of the self-centeredness of modern organizations.

Modern organizations *favor sure gains here* and *now* and *unsure losses far* and *later* while *disfavoring sure losses here* and *now* and *unsure gains far* and *later*. For example, they would rather gain $1,000 here and now for sure and lose $10,000 far and later with a 10 percent chance rather than lose $1,000 here and now for sure and gain $10,000 far and later with a 10 percent chance (Table 1).

Table 1 *Self-centered Choices of Modern Organizations*

	sure, here and now	unsure, far and later
gains	favored	*disfavored*
losses	*disfavored*	favored

The self-centered orientation of modern organizations inevitably leads to environmental destruction and human deprivation.

2 The Principle of Responsibility

The outstanding German-American philosopher *Hans Jonas* has injected the problem of moral responsibility into contemporary moral discourse. Jonas published the German version of his theory of responsibility under the title *Das Prinzip Verantwortung. Versuch einer Ethic für die Technologische Zivilization* (Jonas 1979). The rewritten and enlarged English edition was published under the title *The Imperative of Responsibility: In Search of an Ethics for the Technological Age* (Jonas 1984).

Jonas argues that the nature of human action has changed so dramatically in our times that a correspondingly radical *change* in *ethics* is called for as well. He emphasizes that in previous ethics

> all dealing with the nonhuman world, that is, the whole realm of techne was ethically neutral. Ethical significance belonged to the direct dealing of man with man, including man dealing with himself: all traditional ethics is *anthropocentric*. The entity of 'man' and his basic condition was considered constant in essence and not itself an object of reshaping techne. The effective range of action was small, the time span of foresight, goal-setting, and accountability was short, control of circumstances limited (Jonas 1984: 4–5).

According to Jonas new dimensions of responsibility emerged because *nature* became a subject of human responsibility. This is underscored by the irreversibility and cumulative character of the human impact on the living world. *Knowledge*, under these circumstances, is a prime duty of man and must be commensurate with the causal scale of human action. We should seek "not only the human good but also the good of things extra-human, that is, to extend the recognition of 'ends in themselves' beyond the sphere of man and make the human good include the care of them" (Jonas 1984: 7–8).

For Jonas, an *imperative* responding to the new type of human action might run like this: "Act so that the effects of your actions are compatible with the permanence of genuine human life." Or, expressed negatively: "Act so that the effects of your actions are not destructive to the future possibility of such life" (Jonas 1984: 11).

Jonas argues that our duties to future generations and to nature are independent of any idea of rights or reciprocity. Human responsibility basically consists of a *non-reciprocal duty* to *guarding beings*.

Jonas states that the necessary conditions of moral responsibility are as follows: "The first and most general condition of responsibility is causal power, that is, that acting makes an impact on the world; the second, that such acting is under the agent's control; and the third, that he can foresee its consequences to some extent" (Jonas 1984: 90).

Jonas emphasizes the fact that prospective responsibility is never formal but always *substantive*. "I feel responsible, not in the first place for my conduct and its consequences but for the matter that has a claim on my acting." For example "the well-being, the interest, the fate of others has, by circumstance or by agreement, come to my care, which means that my control over it involves at the same time my obligation to it" (Jonas 1984: 92. and 93.).

Jonas differentiates between *natural responsibility* on the one hand and *contractual responsibility* on the other. "It is the distinction between natural responsibility, where the immanent 'ought-to-be' of the object claims its agent a priori and quite unilaterally, and contracted or appointed responsibility, which is conditional a posteriori upon the fact and the terms of the relationship actually entered into" (Jonas 1984: 95).

The parent and the statesman are presented as ideal types of natural responsibility and contractual responsibility, respectively. The parent is responsible for his or her child not because of the child's own will or even contrary to it. However, the responsibility of the statesman comes from the political contract that he or she has established with his or her constituencies.

There are important similarities between Jonas' theory of responsibility and the ethic of care described by *Carol Gilligan* in her best-seller "In a Different Voice: Psychological Theory and Women's Development" (Gilligan 1982).

Gilligan characterizes the morality of women as an *ethic* of *care*. "The ideal of care is thus an activity of relationship, of seeing and responding to need, taking care of the world by sustaining the web of connection so that no one is left alone." The ethic of care "is the wish not to hurt others and the hope that in morality lies a way of solving conflicts so that no one will be hurt." Women consider the inflicting of hurt as "selfish and immoral in its reflection of unconcern, while the expression of care is seen as fulfillment of moral responsibility" (Gilligan 1982: 62, 65, and 73).

Gilligan states that men and women represent different moral ideologies: the ethic of rights and the ethic of care, respectively. Separation is justified by an ethic of rights while attachment is supported by an ethic of care. "The morality of rights is predicated on equality and centered on the understanding of fairness, while the ethic of responsibility relies on the concept of equity, the recognition of differences in need. While the ethic of rights is a manifestation of equal respect, balancing the claims of other and the self, the ethic of responsibility rests on an understanding that gives rise to compassion and care" (Gilligan 1982: 165).

Gilligan does not argue for the superiority of women's morality. The two disparate modes of moral experience are connected in *mature morality*. "While an ethic of justice proceeds from the premise of equality – that everyone should be treated the same – an ethic of care rests on the premise of non-violence – that no one should be hurt." In maturity "both perspectives converge in the realization that just as inequality adversely affects both parties in an unequal relationship, so too violence is destructive for everyone involved" (Gilligan 1982: 174). An advanced concept of responsibility integrates the reverence for rights represented by men and the non-violence of care represented by women.

3 Making Ethical Decisions

In business context *Kenneth E. Goodpaster* offers the most operationalized model of ethical decision making (Goodpaster 1983).

3.1 Rationality and Respect

Goodpaster proposes understanding moral responsibility as a combination of two basic components, namely rationality and respect.

Rationality involves the following attributes:

(i)   lack of impulsiveness;
(ii)   care in mapping out alternatives and consequences;
(iii) clarity about goals and purposes;
(iv)   attention to details of implementation.

Rationality described by attributes (i),....,(iv) greatly differs from the rationality postulate of mainstream economics that requires consistent utility maximization. The rationality concept used here is *process oriented* and does not require maximizing anything.

Respect is the other component of moral responsibility. For Goodpaster, respect means a special awareness of and concern for the effects of one's decisions and policies on others, beyond seeing others as merely instrumental in accomplishing one's own purposes. This is respect for the lives of others and involves taking their needs and interests seriously, not simply as resources in one's own decision making but as limiting conditions, which change the very definition of one's habitat from a self-centered to a shared environment (Goodpaster and Matthews 1982: 134).

Respect described in this way has a basic similarity to the *altruistic behavior* that is widely discussed in psychology, economics, and sociology. Italian economist *Stefano Zamagni* offers a clear conceptualization of altruistic behavior. He defines individuals as altruistic when they feel and act as if the welfare of others were an end in itself; that is, as something of relevance independently of its effects on their own well-being (Zamagni 1992).

3.2 The 3 R Model

Goodpaster's model is a consequentialist system interwoven with agent-relative elements. *Agent-relativity* means that the model permits the decision maker to produce less than the overall best consequences for the stakeholders in order to realize her or his own goals and purposes. The model also extends to incorporating agent-relative constraints that would simply forbid certain courses of action for the decision maker.

Consequentialist models can be criticized on consequentialist as well as non-consequentialist grounds. In complex economic and political decision situations phenomena can emerge that make the consequentialist evaluation of an act very difficult, if not impossible. The most important of these phenomena are marginal contributions, uncertain consequences, and distant effects.

There are cases where the agent's choice produces only marginally negative consequences to the stakeholders but the cumulative and/or aggregate effect of this kind of behavior is detrimental to them. Ecologist Garret Hardin's famous '*tragedy of the commons*' model describes such situations (Hardin 1968).

If some consequences of an act are rather uncertain then the decision makers tend to neglect them in their consequentialist considerations. This may lead to inadequate accounting. Similarly, if the consequences of an act are distant in space and/or time then the decision makers discount them at a positive (and sometimes very high) rate. Hence consequences beyond the normal space and time reference of the decision makers are usually overdiscounted.

The phenomena of marginal contributions, uncertain consequences, and distant effects present decision traps from which there is no escape within the consequentialist framework.

Consequentialist models are also criticized from a deontological point of view. Deontological ethicists have developed strong deontological arguments that overwrite consequentialist considerations. The decision maker may have deontological reasons not to do certain things even if they would lead to good overall consequences. Deontological reasons limit what we may do to others or how we may treat them (Nagel 1986).

It is better to define respect exclusively in terms of altruistic orientation toward the affected parties. Also, we can introduce deontological considerations as a separate component into the model of ethical decision making. In this way we can get a more robust model in which ethical decision making is characterized by the making of a *synthesis* of *deontological considerations*, *rationality* in *goal-achievement*, and *respect* for the *stakeholders*. This model of ethical decision making can be called the *3 R model*, since its components are reverence & rationality & respect (Zsolnai 1997) (See *Figure 1*).

Ethical Decision Making =

Reverence + Rationality + Respect

Figure 1 *The 3 R Model of Responsibility*

3.3 *Complex Decision Situations*

The following features can characterize complex business or public administration decision situations. First, at least two decision alternatives are available for the decision maker; that is, she or he can choose among different courses of action. Second, in the decision situation ethical norms apply which represent duties of the decision maker. Third, the decision maker has goals that she or he wants to achieve in the decision situation. Finally, different stakeholders are present that can be affected by the outcome of the decision.

We can formalize the above-listed elements of complex decision situations as follows:

(1) A1,...,Ai,...,Am   (m ≥ 2)

This means that at least two decision alternatives are feasible for the decision maker.

(2) D1,...,Dk,...,Dp   (p ≥ 1)

This means that at least one ethical norm applies in the choice situation.

(3) G1,...,Gj,...,Gn $\qquad$ (n ≥ 1)

This means that the decision maker has at least one goal that she or he wants to achieve.

(4) S1,...,Sq,...,Sr $\qquad$ (r ≥ 1)

This means that at least one stakeholder is present in the choice situation.

Ethical decision making involves finding and implementing the decision alternative that best corresponds to the idea of moral responsibility in the given context. Which is the appropriate decision rule for making an ethical decision?

(5) $A^* = \Omega$ (A1,...,Ai,...,Am)

where A* refers to the selected alternative.

Deontological value can be defined as the value of a decision alternative seen from the perspective of the applicable ethical norms. The deontological values of the decision alternatives A1,...,Ai,...,Am can be represented by a vector as follows:

(6) $\underline{d}$ = [D(A1),...,D(Ak),...,D(Am)]

D(Ai) can be measured on the ordinal scale [1, 0, -2]. This means that D(Ai) = 1 if Ai is right regarding the ethical norms; D(Ai) = 0 if Ai is neutral regarding the ethical norms; and D(Ai) = -2 if Ai is wrong regarding the ethical norms.

It is natural that the decision maker considers the value of the decision alternatives with a view toward the achievement of her or his own goals. In classical decision theory this was the only dimension in which courses of action were evaluated and decided upon.

Goal-achievement value can be defined as the value of a decision alternative seen from the locus of the achievement of the decision maker's goals.

The goal-achievement value of the decision alternatives A1,...,Ai,...,Am can be represented by a vector.

(7) $g = [G(A1),...,G(Ai),...,G(Am)]$

$G(Ai)$ is measured on the ordinal scale $[1, 0, -2]$. This means that $G(Ai) = 1$ if Ai is useful regarding the goals; $G(Ai) = 0$ if Ai is neutral regarding the goals; and $G(Ai) = -2$ if Ai is unuseful regarding the goals.

 Stakeholder value can be defined as the value of a decision alternative seen from the perspective of the stakeholders. The stakeholder values of decision alternatives A1,...,Ai,...,Am can be represented by a vector:

(8) $\underline{s} = [S(A1),...,S(Ai),...,S(Am)]$

$S(Ai)$ can be measured on the ordinal scale $[1, 0, -2]$. This means that $S(Ai) = 1$ if Ai is good regarding the stakeholders; $S(Ai) = 0$ if Ai is neutral regarding the stakeholders; and $S(Ai) = -2$ if Ai is bad regarding the stakeholders.

 Holding (6), (7), and (8) together we can get a *multiple evaluation* of the decision alternative Ai.

(9) $\underline{v} = [D(Ai), G(Ai), S(Ai)]$

The first component of the vector is the deontological value of the decision alternative; the second component is the goal-achievement value of the decision alternative, while the third component is the stakeholder value of the decision alternative.

 The vector $\underline{v}$ represents a simultaneous evaluation of the same course of action from different perspectives. The deontological value is assessed from the perspective of an impartial observer; the goal-achievement value is assessed from the perspective of the agent; and the stakeholder value is assessed from the perspective of the affected parties (*Figure 2*).

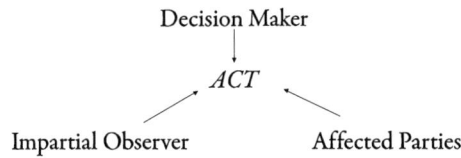

Figure 2 *Multiple Perspectives in Evaluation of an Act*

The "ethical calculus" advanced here is close to Amartya Sen's ideas about the moral evaluation of acts. In his influential book "On Ethics & Economics" he writes: "To get an overall assessment of the ethical standing of an activity it is necessary not only to look at its own intrinsic value (if any), but also its instrumental role and its consequences on other things" (Sen 1987: 75). Our moral accounting system tries to do this job.

3.4 The Maximin Principle

A matrix that contains multiple evaluations of all the decision alternatives available for the decision maker can provide an overall picture about the choice situation.

$$
(10)\quad \underline{V} =
\begin{matrix}
D(A1),.....,G(A1),....,S(A1) \\
\cdot\qquad\quad \cdot\qquad\quad \cdot \\
D(Ai),.....,G(Ai),.....,S(Ai) \\
\cdot\qquad\quad \cdot\qquad\quad \cdot \\
D(Am),....,G(Am),...,S(Am)
\end{matrix}
$$

The matrix $\underline{V}$ may present *value conflict*. The best strategy is to maintain the complexity of the decision situation and try to find an *optimal compromise* among diverse value dimensions. Trying to balance different values against one another is an essential strategy in complex choice situations. The *maximin rule* can do the required job well. It implies the maximization of the minimum payoff of decision alternatives.

Austrian logician *Earnest Zermello* first described the maximin rule in 1912. In his groundbreaking "Theory of Games and Economic Behavior", Hungarian-American mathematician *John Von Neumann* developed the rule further (Von Neumann and Morgenstein 1944).

In complex decision situations the *rule* of *making ethical decisions* is stated as follows:

(11) $A^* = \text{maximin } [D(Ai), G(Ai), S(Ai)]$

It demands the selection of the *least worst alternative* in the decision space of deontological, goal-achievement, and stakeholder values – in the sense that the minimum value of the selected alternative is greater than the minimum value of any other alternative available for the decision maker in the given situation. The comparability of $D(Ai)$, $G(Ai)$, and $S(Ai)$ is provided by the fact that they are measured on the same ordinal scale $[1, 0, -2]$.

If there are two decision alternatives A1 and A2, then the responsible decision is A1 if and only if:

(12) $\text{min } [D(A1), G(A1), S(A1)] > \text{min } [D(A2), G(A2), S(A2)]$

The underlying principle of responsible decision making is that the decision maker should find an optimal compromise among the applicable ethical norms, the achievable goals, and the interests of the stakeholders.

The ethical decision defined by (11) provides a *Pareto optimal result* in the multidimensional decision space. This means that given the set of decision alternatives it is not possible to increase their value in one value dimension without decreasing their value in at least one other value dimension.

4 Analyzing the World Bank Case

A provocative case concerning the *World Bank environmental policy* is useful in demonstrating how the ethical decision-making model works.

In the early 1990s, some economic advisors of the World Bank were proposing that the organization should encourage increased migration of dirty industries to less-developed countries. The argument was as follows:

> The measurement of the costs of health-impairing pollution depends on the fore-gone earnings from increased morbidity and mortality. From this point of view a given amount of health-impairing pollution should be done in the country with the lowest cost, which will be the country with the lowest wages (...) The costs of pollution are likely to be non-linear as the initial increments of pollution probably have very low cost ... The demand for a clean environment for aesthetic and health reasons is likely to have very high income-elasticity. The concern over an agent that causes a one-in-a-million in the odds of the prostate cancer is obviously going to be much higher in a country where people survive to get prostate cancer than in a country where under-5 mortality is 200 per thousand. Also, much of the concern over industrial atmospheric discharge is about visibility-impairing particulates. These discharges may have very little health impact. Clearly, trade in goods that embody aesthetic pollution concerns could be welfare enchanting (The Economist 1992: 66).

In this case, there are a variety of stakeholders because not only citizens of developed and less-developed countries are affected by the World Bank environmental policy, but also the natural environment and future generations. The policy options (alternatives) are as follows:

A1 = encouraging the migration of dirty industries to LDCs
A2 = not encouraging the migration of dirty industries to LDCs

The most relevant ethical norm that applies here is fairness (D). It is formulated by *Hausman* and *McPherson* as the pay-your-way principle, which requires locating dirty industries so that those who derive the largest benefits from industries endure most of the pollution costs (Hausman and McPherson 1996: 204).

The declared goal of the World Bank is to enhance global welfare (G).

The most important stakeholders can be identified as citizens of the developed countries (S1), dirty industries in the developed countries (S2), citizens of the less-developed countries (S3), the natural environment affected by dirty industries in the developed countries (S4), the targeted natural environment in the less-developed countries (S5), and future generations (S6).

From a deontological perspective alternative A1 is certainly wrong while alternative A2 is certainly right because the latter corresponds to the norm of fairness and the former violates it. Using the ordinal scale of [1, 0, -2] we can calculate the deontological values of A1 and A2 as follows:

$$D(A1) = -2$$
$$D(A2) = 1$$

Alternative A1 can be useful for the goal of enchanting global welfare with probability p. Alternative A2 might be useless for the achievement of this goal with probability q. Using the ordinal scale of [1, 0, -2] we can calculate the goal-achievement values of A1 and A2 as follows:

$$G(A1) = 1(p) -2 (1-p) = 3p -2$$
$$G(A2) = 1(1-q) -2 (q) = 1 -3q$$

Migration of dirty industries to LDCs would be good for the citizens of developed countries (S1), for the industries themselves (S2), and for the natural environment affected by those industries in the developed countries (S4). However, it would be bad for the citizens of less-developed countries (S3), for the targeted natural environment in the less-developed countries (S5), and for future generations (S6) since environmental pollution is much more controllable in the developed countries than in the less-developed countries.

Using the ordinal scale [1, 0, -2] the stakeholder values of A1 can be calculated as follows:

$$S1(A1) = 1$$
$$S2(A1) = 1$$
$$S3(A1) = -2$$
$$S4(A1) = 1$$
$$S5(A1) = -2$$
$$S6(A1) = -2$$

A2 is neutral for stakeholders S1,...,S5 since it does not change the present status quo. However, future generations (S6) could *benefit* from keeping dirty industries in the developed countries by forcing them to innovate and to become more environmentally friendly.

For this reason the stakeholder values of alternative A2 can be calculated as follows:

$$S1(A2) = 0$$
$$S2(A2) = 0$$
$$S3(A2) = 0$$
$$S4(A2) = 0$$
$$S5(A2) = 0$$
$$S6(A1) = 1$$

The question remaining is how to weight stakeholders S1,...,S6:

Let v1,...,v6 be importance weights attributed to the stakeholders. On the basis of inter-species and inter-generational justice we can argue that equal weights should be attributed to nature, society, and future generations. This implies that v1 + v2 + v3 = v4 + v5 = v6. We do not discriminate between citizens of the developed countries and citizens of the less-developed countries, consequently v1 = v3. Similarly, we do not discriminate between the natural environment in the developed countries and the natural environment in the less-developed countries, consequently v4 = v5. Considering that almost everybody is served by dirty industries, they can get a weight similar to citizens of the developed countries: v1 = v2.

It is required that

$$\sum vi = 1 \qquad (i = 1,...,6)$$

Hence we get

$$v1 = 1/9; v2 = 1/9; v3 = 1/9; v4 = 1/6; v5 = 1/6; v6 = 1/3$$

Aggregate stakeholder values of the two alternatives are as follows:

$$S(A1) = -5/6 \approx -0{,}83$$
$$S(A2) = 1/3 \approx 0{,}33$$

Table 2 shows the different values of the two policy options.

Table 2 *Values in the World Bank Case*

	deontological value	goal-achievement value	stakeholder value
A1 alternative	-2	3p −2	-0,83
A2 alternative	1	1 − 3q	0,33

Multiple evaluations of the alternatives are provided by the following vectors:

$$V(A1) = [-2, 3p-2, -0{,}83]$$
$$V(A2) = [1, 1-3q, 0{,}33]$$

According to the maximin rule A2 is better than A1 since min V(A2) > min V(A1). The worst component of V(A1) is −2 while the worst component of V(A2) is greater than -2 (holding that 1 > q > 0 and hence 1 -3q > -2).

The World Bank *should not encourage migration* of *dirty industries* to less-developed countries. Encouraging migration of dirty industries to less-developed countries is unacceptable from the deontological perspective and also negative from the stakeholder perspective, so some questionable welfare improvement cannot compensate for the violation of ethical norms and vital stakeholder interests.

5 Conclusions

The *procedural model* of ethical decision making can be summarized as follows:

(I)   Framing of the decision situation by
      (i)   identifying the applicable ethical norms;
      (ii) mapping out the affected parties;
      (iii) defining goals and generating alternatives.

(II)   Multiple evaluation of the available alternatives regarding
      (i)   the ethical norms;
      (ii) the goals to be achieved;
      (iii) the affected parties.

(III) Finding the least worst alternative in the multidimensional space of deontological, goal-achievement, and stakeholder values.

The ethical decision maker can be characterized as having the ability to take *multiple perspectives* and make *optimal balances* across diverse value dimensions. He or she is a properly socialized individual who has developed *reflexivity* regarding the *ethical norms* of her or his society and displays *empathy* toward *others*.

Perverse decisions of modern organizations can be avoided by employing ethical decision making. The preservation of the natural environment and the provision of the good life for present and future generations require *critical sensitivity* to the ethical norms of society and *caring* for human and non-human beings.

References

Dawes, R.M., Van de Kragt, A.J.C. and Orbell, J.M. (1990), "Cooperation for the Benefit of Us – Not Me, or My Conscience" in J.J. Mansbridge (Ed.): *Beyond Self-Interest*, The University of Chicago Press, Chicago & London, pp. 97–110.

Goodpaster, K.E. (1983), "The Concept of Corporate Responsibility," *Journal of Business Ethics*, 1983(1), pp. 1–22.

Goodpaster, K.E. and Matthews, J.B. (1982), "Can a Corporation Have Conscience?" *Harvard Business Review*, 1982. (1), pp. 132–141.

Hardin, G. (1968), "The Tragedy of the Commons" *Science*, 1968 (December), pp. 1243–1248.

Jonas, H. (1984), *The Imperative of Responsibility: In Search of an Ethics for the Technological Age*, The University of Chicago Press, Chicago & London.

Kahneman, D. and Tversky, A. (1979), "Prospect Theory: An Analysis of Decision Under Risk," *Econometrica*, 1979 (March), pp. 263–291.

Nagel, T. (1986), *A View from Nowhere*, Oxford University Press, New York.

von Neuman, J. and Morgenstein, O. (1944), *Theory of Games and Economic Behavior*, Princeton University Press, Princeton.

Sen, A. (1987), *On Ethics and Economics*, Blackwell, Oxford.

Sing, J.B. and Lakhan, V.C. (1989), "Business Ethics and the International Trade in Hazardous Wastes," *Journal of Business Ethics*, 1989 (2).

Walzer, M. (1993), *The Spheres of Justice*, Basic Books, New York.

Zamagni, S. (Ed.) (1992), *Economics of Altruism*. Edward Elgar, Chettelham.

Zsolnai, L. (1997), *Responsibility and Choice: Decision Making in Multiple Value Perspectives*, The Netherlands Institute for Advanced Study, Wassenaar (Manuscript).

CHAPTER 5

Beyond Competitiveness:
Creating Values for a Sustainable World*

> There must be no competition among you, no conceit ... Always consider
> the other person to be better than yourself, so that nobody thinks of his
> own interests first but everybody thinks of other people's interests instead.
> — *Philippians* 2: 3–4

Economics is rightly called a 'dismal science'. It propagates a negativistic
view of human nature. In this view economic agents are always self-interested and want to maximize their own profit or utility. Their interactions
are based on competition only and their criterion of success is growth
measured in money terms. Mainstream economics generates vicious circles
in which market players expect the worst from others and act accordingly.
Competitive economics produces an enormous abundance of goods and
services but at an intolerable environmental and social cost.

*   First published: "Beyond Competitiveness: Creating Values for a Sustainable World"
     in A. Tencati and L. Zsolnai (Eds): *The Collaborative Enterprise – Creating Values
     for a Sustainable World*. Oxford, Bern & Berlin: 2010. Peter Lang. pp. 575–588
     (Co-author: *Antonio Tencati*).

1 Competitiveness versus Collaboration

If we want to get closer to a sustainable world we need to generate *virtuous circles* in economic life where good dispositions, good behavior and good expectations reinforce each other. Our *collaborative enterprise project* (Tencati and Zsolnai 2000) promotes a view in which economic agents care about others and themselves and aim to create values for all the participants in their business ecosystems. Their criterion of success is mutually satisfying relationships with the stakeholders.

The contrasting characteristics of the competitive and collaborative models are summarized in *Table 1*.

Table 1 *Competitiveness versus Collaboration*

	The Competitive Model	The Collaborative Model
Basic motive	self-interest	care about others and oneself
Main goal	maximizing profit or shareholder value	creating values for all the participants in the network
Criterion of success	growth in money terms	mutually beneficial relationships with the stakeholders

2 Positive Psychology and the 'Homo Reciprocans' Model

The skeptics, including most economists, may believe that the premises of the collaborative model are naive. Recent discoveries in social sciences suggest that this is not the case.

A new branch of psychology called *positive psychology*, initiated by *Martin Seligman* and *Mihaly Csikszentmihalyi*, studies the strengths and virtues that allow individuals, communities, and societies to thrive (Positive Psychology Center 2007; Seligham and Csikszentmihalyi 2000).

Positive psychology has been defined as a science of positive subjective experience, positive individual traits, and positive institutions (Seligham and Csikszentmihalyi 2000), which aims at improving quality of life and preventing the pathologies caused by a barren and meaningless way of living. Positive psychologists try to improve everyday well-being, to make life worth living. As a supplement to the vast research on the disorders and their treatment, they suggest that there should be an equally thorough study of strengths and virtues, and that they should work towards developing interventions that can help people become lastingly happier (Seligman, Parks and Steen 2004).

Positive psychology focuses on three different routes to happiness (Seligman 2002; Seligman, Steen, Park and Peterson 2005):

(i) *Positive emotion* and *pleasure* (the pleasant life). This is a hedonic approach, which deals with increasing positive emotions as part of normal and healthy life. "Within limits, we can increase our positive emotion about the past (e.g. by cultivating gratitude and forgiveness), our positive emotion about the present (e.g. by savouring and mindfulness) and our positive emotion about the future (e.g. by building hope and optimism)" (Seligman, Parks and Steen 2004).

(ii) *Engagement* (the engaged life). This constituent of happiness is not merely hedonic but regards the pursuit of gratification (Seligman, Parks and Steen, 2004). In order to achieve this goal, a person should involve himself/herself fully by drawing upon "character strengths such as creativity, social intelligence, sense of humour, perseverance, and an appreciation of beauty and excellence" (Seligman, Parks and Steen 2004). This leads to beneficial experiences of immersion, absorption, and flow.

(iii) *Meaning* (the meaningful life). This calls for a deeper involvement of an individual, using the character strengths to belong to and serve something larger and more permanent than the self: "something such as as knowledge, goodness, family, community, politics, justice or a higher spiritual power" (Seligman, Parks and Steen 2004).

Peterson and Seligman developed the so-called *Character Strengths and Virtues* framework, which identifies and classifies strengths and virtues that enable human flourishing. It lists six overarching virtues, common to almost every culture in the world, made up of 24 measurable character strengths. The classification of these virtues and strengths is as follows (Peterson and Seligman 2004; Seligman, Steen, Park and Peterson 2005):

(1) *Wisdom and Knowledge*: creativity, curiosity, open-mindedness, love of learning, perspective;
(2) *Courage*: authenticity, bravery, persistence, zest;
(3) *Humanity*: kindness, love, social intelligence;
(4) *Justice*: fairness, leadership, teamwork;
(5) *Temperance*: forgiveness, modesty, prudence, self-regulation;
(6) *Transcendence*: appreciation of beauty and excellence, gratitude, hope, humor, religiousness.

What we need in business and economics is a commitment to helping individuals and organizations identify their strengths and use them to increase and sustain the well-being of others and themselves.

One of the most exciting developments in the behavioral and social sciences is the emergence of the so-called *Homo reciprocans* model as a major alternative to the model of *Homo oeconomicus* propagated by mainstream economics and business. The Homo oeconomicus model suggests that economic agents are exclusively self-interested and always maximize their utility functions. Overwhelming empirical evidence shows that this is a rather unrealistic description of human behavior. The model has also been criticized on various normative grounds (Zsolnai 2002a).

Samuel Bowles, Robert Boyd, Ernst Fehr, and *Herbert Gintis* summarize the emerging model of Homo reciprocans as follows. Homo reciprocans comes to new social situations with a propensity to cooperate and share, responds to cooperative behavior by maintaining or increasing his or her level of cooperation, and responds to selfish, free-riding behavior by retaliating against the offenders, even at a cost to himself/herself, and even when he or she could not reasonably expect future personal gains from such retaliation (Bowles, Boyd, Fehr and Gintis 1997). This is certainly in line with empirical observations: people do produce public goods, they do observe normative restraints on the pursuit of self-interest (even when there is nobody watching), and they will put themselves to a lot of trouble to hurt rule breakers.

Robert Frank's research shows that socially responsible firms can survive in competitive environments because social responsibility brings substantial benefits for them. Frank identifies five distinct types of cases where socially responsible organizations are rewarded for the higher cost of caring: (i) opportunistic behavior can be avoided between owners and managers, (ii) moral satisfaction induces employees to work more for lower salaries, (iii) high quality new employees can be recruited, (iv) customers' loyalty can be gained, and (v) the trust of subcontractors can be established. In this way caring organizations are rewarded for the higher costs of socially responsible behavior by their ability to form commitments among owners, managers and employees and to establish trust relationships with customers and subcontractors (Frank 2004).

These findings give us the hope that noble efforts of economic agents are acknowledged and reciprocated even in highly competitive markets. Institutions and individual behavior co-evolve in social interactions and shape the evolution of individual preferences. In turn, these preferences shape the overall evolution, and may lead to the emergence of new economic organizations (Shalizi 1999).

3 Issues for Future Research

Our work is a first step in a research track to reframe current behavioral and institutional patterns in economics and business practices. In our book *The Collaborative Enterprise* (Tencati and Zsolnai 2000) we have collected theoretical contributions, reflections, cases, examples, and initiatives to provide an overview of the topic of collaboration.

The collaborative model opens new research avenues at different levels: at the level of the individual; the level of the firm; the level of districts, clusters, industries and sectors; and the level of the economy as a whole.

3.1 Individual level

The new paradigm represented by the Homo reciprocans model is a major challenge to the mainstream competitive model. We need further studies and empirical support to revise and replace the current behavioral bases of economics. A new positive vision of the individual is strongly needed. Positive psychology, anthropology and biology (see, for example, Tomasello 2009), and neuroeconomics (see Camerer, Loewenstein and Prelec 2005) could provide important contributions to reframe the currently dominating negativistic view of human beings.

3.2 Micro level

The firm is the main focus and the starting point of our collaborative enterprise project. The sustainability challenge calls for innovative business and managerial models to combine different values and value dimensions (Zsolnai and Tencati 2009). Creating values for the different constituencies through creativity, broad stakeholder engagement and more balanced and democratic mechanisms of governance is characteristic of the most innovative enterprises. These dispositions also make them more resilient and long-lasting. With regard to the micro level, it is important to study the enabling conditions in terms of institutions, culture, values, managerial approaches, and so on (Campbell 2007), that allow collaborative enterprises to flourish. Furthermore, we think that especially the studies on small and medium-size companies could provide interesting and widespread examples of progressive, locally based and community-rooted practices (Spence 2007).

3.3 Meso level

The collaborative model considers the firm as part of a broader ecosystem, that is, a stakeholder network of which the firm is one of the components. Therefore, the study of these aggregations, especially at the territorial level, becomes critical. Industrial districts (Becattini 1990; Becattini 2004) and clusters (Ketels, Lindqvist and Sölvell 2008; Porter 1998a; Sölvell 2009) are based on the symbiosis between the economic dimension and the social one. In these forms of organization the economic activities are fundamental to boosting the local development (Becattini, Bellandi, Dei Ottati and Sforzi 2003) and, in parallel, the social capital (Bourdieu 1986; Putnam 1993; 2000). Social capital, which connects the local communities and the industries, is one of the most important drivers that explain the long-term success of the involved firms on the market (Porter 1998b). Furthermore, broader networks emerge at the industry and sector level to address sustainability and competitive issues (consider, for example, the waste management policies and the building of industrial ecosystems: Tencati and Perrini 2006; Tukker, Charter, Vezzol, Stø and Andersen 2008). Sustainability and competitive dynamics are no longer matters that can be addressed by isolated and single players. The sustainability goals need broader models of governance. Competition emerges among collaborative networks composed of different actors (Zadek 2006; Zadek, Sabapathy, Døssing and Swift 2003).

It is also interesting to consider the inputs provided by organization studies. According to Ronfeldt, after tribes, hierarchical institutions, and markets, collaborative networks are the emerging form of organization, which affects the current stage of social evolution. "Enabled by the digital information-technology revolution, this form is only now coming into its own, so far strengthening civil society more than other realms" (Ronfeldt 2009). In particular, this framework could also be applied to understanding meaningful evolutions enabled by the information and communication technologies such as the social networks and the online collaborative platforms (Bielli and Nemeslaki 2009).

3.4 Macro level

The current pattern of global development is not only socially and ecologically but also economically unbearable. This calls for enlarged, more
participating models of governance to address the sustainability challenge,
and for the construction of decentralized community-based initiatives
connected in global networks, which could constitute feasible and fitting
alternatives to the global mainstream.

From the relational state perspective (Albareda, Lozano, Tencati,
Perrini and Midttun 2009) we can observe the institutionalization of global
action networks such as the Global Compact, the Global Water Partnership,
The Forest and the Marine Stewardship Councils, the Global Reporting
Initiative, the Microcredit Summit Campaign, the International Federation
of Organic Agriculture Movements and the Fair Labor Association, which
operate in both environmental and social realms (Glasbergen 2010; Global
Action Network Net 2010). They can be described as "civil society initiated multi-stakeholder arrangements that aim to fulfil a leadership role
for systemic change in global governance for sustainable development"
(Glasbergen 2010: 130). In these new forms of partnership collaborative
efforts are carried on jointly by governments/public institutions, firms and
civil society organizations. Therefore, the collaborative model is gaining
ground in the political arena with solutions, trying to overcome the conventional public-private partnerships.

The collaborative networks enable local communities to become
innovative players on the global scene. Therefore, it is crucial to study the
emergence of new patterns of governance where coalitions of global players
and global alliances of local actors interact to address disequilibria in economic, social and ecological conditions. A deeper analysis of collaborative
models of governance is also needed when they arise to manage the paths
of development at local, national and regional levels (Albareda, Lozano,
Tencati, Midttun and Perrini 2008).

4 Conclusion

The previous reflections define a research agenda focused on the different features and implications of the collaborative model. However, a conclusive remark is needed. We do not want to neglect the important economic and social role played by competition. What we consider unacceptable is that *competition* – one of the possible tools to advance human well-being and societal welfare – has become the *only criterion* to rule economic and social life. We are against glorifying economic competition as an end in itself because it leads to detrimental effects on nature, society and future generations (Zsolnai 2009).

We believe that economic players need to go beyond competition to build a progressive economics. Business should respect the ecological and social limits in which it operates, and embed its activities in the natural and social systems (Zsolnai 2002b).

References

Albareda, L., Lozano, J.M., Tencati, A., Midttun, A., and Perrini, F. (2008), "The Changing Role of Governments in Corporate Social Responsibility: Drivers and Responses," *Business Ethics: A European Review* 17(4), pp. 347–363.

Albareda, L., Lozano, J.M., Tencati, A., Perrini, F., and Midttun, A. (2009), "The Role of Government in Corporate Social Responsibility," in Zsolnai, L., Boda, Z., Fekete, L. (Eds), *Ethical Prospects: Economy, Society, and Environment* (Springer, Dordrecht, the Netherlands), pp. 103–149.

Becattini, G. (1990), "The Marshallian Industrial District as a Socio-Economic Notion," in Pyke, F., Becattini, G., Sengenberger, W. (Eds), *Industrial Districts and Inter-Firm Co-operation in Italy* (International Institute for Labour Studies, Geneva), pp. 37–51.

Becattini, G. (2004), *Industrial Districts: A New Approach to Industrial Change.* Edward Elgar, Cheltenham.

Becattini, G., Bellandi, M., Dei Ottati, G. and Sforzi, F. (2003), *From Industrial Districts to Local Development: An Itinerary of Research*. Edward Elgar, Cheltenham.

Bielli, P. and Nemeslaki, A. (2009), "Reinventing Organizations with Information and Communication Technologies," in Zsolnai, L. and Tencati, A. (Eds), *The Future International Manager: A Vision of the Roles and Duties of Management*. Palgrave Macmillan, Houndmills, New York, pp. 94–115.

Bourdieu, P.: (1986), "The Forms of Capital," in Richardson J.G. (Ed.), *Handbook of Theory and Research for the Sociology of Education*. Greenwood Press, Westport, CN, pp. 241–258.

Bowles, S., Boyd, R., Fehr, E., and Gintis, H. (1997), *Homo reciprocans: A Research Initiative on the Origins, Dimensions, and Policy Implications of Reciprocal Fairness* (Research Initiative on Reciprocal Fairness, June 7), http://www.umass.edu/preferen/gintis/homo.pdf. (accessed 15/01/2013).

Camerer, C., Loewenstein, G., and Prelec, D. (2005), "Neuroeconomics: How Neuroscience Can Inform Economics," *Journal of Economic Literature* 43 (1), pp. 9–64.

Campbell, J.L. (2007), "Why Would Corporations Behave in Socially Responsible Ways? An Institutional Theory of Corporate Social Responsibility," *Academy of Management Review* 32(3), pp. 946–967.

Frank, R. (2004), *What Price the Moral High Ground? Ethical Dilemmas in Competitive Environments* (Princeton University Press, Princeton, Oxford).

Glasbergen, P. (2010), "Global Action Networks: Agents for Collective Action," *Global Environmental Change* 20(1), pp. 130–141.

Global Action Network Net (2010), *Global Action Networks and GAN-Net*, http://www.scalingimpact.net/gan (accessed 15/01/2013).

Ketels, C., Lindqvist, G., and Sölvell, Ö. (2008), *Clusters and Cluster Initiatives*. Stockholm School of Economics, Stockholm.

Peterson, C., and Seligman, M.E.P. (2004), *Character Strengths and Virtues: A Handbook and Classification*. APA Press and Oxford University Press, Washington D.C.

Porter, M.E. (1998a) *The Competitive Advantage of Nations. New Edition*. Palgrave, New York.

Porter, M.E. (1998b), "Clusters and the New Economics of Competition," *Harvard Business Review* 76 (6), 77–90.

Positive Psychology Center (2007), http://www.ppc.sas.upenn.edu/ (accessed 15/01/2013).

Putnam, R.D. (1993), *Making Democracy Work: Civic Traditions in Modern Italy*. Princeton University Press, Princeton, NJ.

Putnam, R.D. (2000), *Bowling Alone: The Collapse and Revival of American Community*. Simon & Schuster, New York.

Ronfeldt, D. (2009), *Overview of social evolution (past, present, and future) in TIMN Terms*, http://twotheories.blogspot.com/2009/02/overview-of-social-evolution-past.html.

Seligman, M.E.P. (2002), *Authentic Happiness: Using the New Positive Psychology to Realize Your Potential for Lasting Fulfillment*. Free Press, New York.

Seligman, M.E.P. and Csikszentmihalyi, M. (2000), "Positive Psychology: An Introduction," *American Psychologist* 55(1), 5–14.

Seligman, M.E.P., Parks, A.C. and Steen, T. (2004), "A Balanced Psychology and a Full Life," *The Royal Society, Philosophical Transactions: Biological Sciences* 359, 1379–1381.

Seligman, M.E.P., Steen, T.A., Park, N. and Peterson, C. (2005), "Positive Psychology Progress: Empirical Validation of Interventions," *American Psychologist* 60(5), 410–421.

Shalizi, C.R. (1999), "Homo Reciprocans. Political Economy and Cultural Evolution," *Santa Fe Institute Bulletin* 14(2) (Fall), 16–20.

Sölvell, Ö. (2009), *Clusters – Balancing Evolutionary and Constructive Forces. Second Edition*. Ivory Tower Publishers, Stockholm, http://www.cluster-research.org/ (accessed 15/01/2013).

Spence, L.J. (2007), "CSR and Small Business in a European Policy Context: The Five 'C's of CSR and Small Business Research Agenda 2007," *Business and Society Review* 112(4), 533–552.

Tencati, A. and Perrini, F. (2006), "The Sustainability Perspective: A New Governance Model," in Kakabadse, A. and Morsing, M. (Eds), *Corporate Social Responsibility: Reconciling Aspiration with Application* (Palgrave Macmillan, Houndmills, New York), pp. 94–111.

Tencati, A. and Zsolnai, L. (Eds) 2010: *The Collaborative Enterprise – Creating Values for a Sustainable World*. Peter Lang, Oxford, Bern & Berlin.

Tomasello, M. (2009), *Why We Cooperate*. MIT Press, Cambridge, MA.

Tukker, A., Charter, M., Vezzoli, C., Stø, E. and Andersen, M.M. (Eds): 2008, *System Innovation for Sustainability 1. Perspectives on Radical Changes to Sustainable Consumption and Production*. Greenleaf Publishing, Sheffield.

Zadek, S. (2006), "The Logic of Collaborative Governance: Corporate Responsibility, Accountability, and the Social Contract," *Corporate Social Responsibility Initiative Working Paper*, 17. John F. Kennedy School of Government, Harvard University, Cambridge, MA, http://www.ksg.harvard.edu/m-rcbg/CSRI/publications/workingpaper_17_zadek.pdf (accessed 15/01/2013).

Zadek, S., Sabapathy, J., Døssing, H. and Swift, T. (2003), *Responsible Competitiveness: Corporate Responsibility Clusters in Action*. The Copenhagen Centre & AccountAbility, Copenhagen, London.

Zsolnai, L. (2002a), "The Moral Economic Man," in Zsolnai, L. (Ed.), *Ethics in the Economy. Handbook of Business Ethics*. Peter Lang, Oxford, Bern), pp. 39–58.

Zsolnai, L. (2002b), "Future of Capitalism," in Zsolnai, L. (Ed.), *Ethics in the Economy. Handbook of Business Ethics*. Peter Lang, Oxford, Bern), pp. 295–308.

Zsolnai, L. (2009), "Nature, Society and Future Generations," in de Bettignies, H.-C., Lépinueux, F. (Eds), *Business, Globalization and the Common Good* (Peter Lang, Oxford, Bern), pp. 139–152.

Zsolnai, L. and Tencati, A. (Eds) (2009), *The Future International Manager: A Vision of the Roles and Duties of Management*. Palgrave Macmillan, Houndmills, New York.

PART 3

Spirituality in Economics

CHAPTER 6

Ethics Needs Spirituality*

In this paper I argue that ethics needs spirituality as an underlying background and major motivational force.

1 Ethical Motivation and Spirituality

Western ethics suggests that ethical action is a cognitive enterprise. Western ethical theories provide abstract models to be applied or followed by moral agents (deontology, consequentialism, virtue ethics). But we know from practice that the main problem in order to behave ethically is not knowledge but motivation. We should focus on the exercise of moral agency stressed by Stanford psychologist Albert Bandura (1991).

This is where *spirituality* and *transpersonal psychology* can help. If we want to improve the ethicality of our decisions and actions we should enhance the development of our self toward a more inclusive, holistic, and peaceful consciousness. Empirical evidence suggests that spiritual experiences help the person to transcend his or her narrow self-conception and enable him or her to exercise genuine empathy with others and to take an all-encompassing perspective.

Transpersonal psychologist Stanislav Grof (1998) recorded more than thirty thousand spiritual experiences. These include psychedelic therapy, where the non-ordinary states of consciousness are induced by chemical

---

*   First published: "Ethics Needs Spirituality" *Ethics Matters* (Online Magazine of the Center for Business Ethics at Bentley College, Mass., USA) June 2006. pp. 1–5.

means; spiritual emergencies, which develop spontaneously for unknown reasons in the midst of everyday life; and holotropic breathwork, which is facilitated by a combination of faster breathing, evocative music, and a specific form of focused body work. These spiritual experiences involve "authentic experimental identification with other people, animals, plants and various other aspects of nature and cosmos." (...) "We typically undergo profound changes in our understanding of existence and of the nature of reality. We directly experience the divine, sacred, or numinous dimensions of existence in a compelling way." (Grof 1998: 2 and 17).

Despite the rich diversity of spiritual experience, the main ethical message is always the same: love and compassion, deep reverence for life, and empathy with all sentient beings. Grof summarizes the result of spiritual experiences as follows: "We develop a new system of values that is not based on conventional norms, precepts, commandments, and fear of punishment, but on our knowledge and understanding of the universal order. We realize that we are an integral part of creation and that by hurting others we would be hurting ourselves." (Grof 1998: 129).

2 Spiritually-based Leadership

Spirituality offers rich implications for management and leadership. As Josep Lozano and Raimon Ribera observe, the way we manage depends on the way we are. Spirituality is not something that we can just tack on to management: if spirituality is in our nature, we will bring it with us when we manage. The question is what type of management results from placing spirituality at the core of the human condition. They write:

> Management is a challenge for spirituality. The connection is not automatic; it needs effort and vigilance to develop. Management practices generate feedback that impacts our own vision of life, humanity and spirituality. Management benefits from an approach that does not merely consider spirituality as a potential 'addition' to management. The opportunity should be seized to develop a more precise, richer conception of management. (Lozano and Ribera 2004: 175)

Peter Pruzan notes that the term 'management', as traditionally conceived, includes such activities as strategy, planning, administration, and control. In recent years, particularly in the West, the term 'management' has been supplemented with the term 'leadership'. This later term is now being used to relate to concepts, processes, and roles that had not previously been central to the traditional themes of management. These include such notions as corporate vision, change-management, stakeholder-dialogue, and social and ethical accountability in self-organizing and values-based organizations (Pruzan 2004: 16).

Luk Bouckaert (2004) warns that while a manager thinks through instrumental rationality, a leader is driven by a more intrinsic and contagious commitment to values. But the cult of leadership, fostered by spirituality, has an ambiguous record. It is rooted in a long history of aristocratic, hierarchic, and authoritarian tradition.

Plato created the figure of the philosopher king, who combines power and wisdom, to represent the ideal leader. For Plato spirituality is an intellectual and emotional search for inner enlightenment, realized in our soul through recollecting the genuine forms (ideas) of life. Physical, mental, and spiritual training is needed (and was provided in Plato's Academia) to achieve enlightenment and become a good leader. The philosopher king is the cornerstone of Plato's aristocratic philosophy of governance. We should question the links among spirituality, leadership, and aristocracy observed in many religious organizations and possibly extending to other organizations. Promoting leadership should not be connected with a hidden sympathy for a system of economic aristocracy and the control of people (Bouckaert 2004: 51).

There might be no contradiction between management and leadership. Perhaps one can refer to a 'mutation' in the organizational evolution that is proving to be advantageous for individual and organizational survival: the hybrid leader-manager who masters both leading and managing. Spirituality presents a humanistic, democratic, and sustainable frame of reference for the behavior of leader-managers and their organizations.

Lozano and Ribera (2004) argue that spirituality can be a source of quality for the individual and for society. But it can also be a source of quality for the organization. Indeed, this is one of the key challenges of our time. This becomes relevant in a context where society is undergoing permanent change and corporations are becoming knowledge organizations or learning organizations. If knowledge is the key asset, then developing a human quality must lie at the heart of the corporate structure. Therefore, organizational criteria should ensure that human resources work smoothly and are constantly enhanced.

What do we mean by 'the quality of an organization'? A quality organization can infuse the individuals who comprise it with purpose and enthusiasm rather than exploiting and manipulating them. Such an organization fosters the following (Lozano and Ribera 2004: 179).

(i)   the personal quality of the organization members;
(ii)   the professional responsibility of the organization members;
(iii) the quality of the relations among the organization members;
(iv)   the quality of the organization's products;
(v)   the quality of organizational processes;
(vi)   the statement, development, and embodiment of values;
(vii) active partnerships with stakeholders (customers, employees, shareholders, suppliers, plus others directly affected by the company's activities).

3 Why Ethics Needs Spirituality

The well-being of human communities, natural ecosystems, and future generations requires authentic care, which may develop from experiential oneness with others and with the universal source of creation.

Ethics might be seen as a process of self-realization. Oxford-based thinker Danah Zohar speaks about *spiritual intelligence*. It is a transformative intelligence, which makes us ask basic questions of meaning, purpose, and values. Spiritual intelligence allows us to understand situations and systems deeply, to invent new categories, to be creative and go beyond the given paradigms (Zohar 2002: 303).

I do not want to argue that we should cultivate spirituality for improving the ethicality of our actions. Spirituality is a value in itself, a major gift in our life. It is a positive by-product of spirituality that it can provide us with high-level ethical motivation. But if spirituality is used instrumentally then its value will be lost and the consequences will be destructive. There are no tricks in ethics: "As inside, so outside."

References

Bandura, A. (1991), "Social cognitive theory of moral thought and action" in W.M. Kurtines and J.L. Gewirtz (Eds): *Handbook of Moral Behavior and Development. Theory, Research and Applications*. Erlbaum, Hillsdale, NJ. Vol. 1. pp. 71–129.

Bouckaert, L. (2004), "Spirituality and Economic Democracy" in L. Zsolnai (Ed): *Spirituality and Ethics in Management*. Kluwer Academic Publishers, Boston, Dordrecht & London. pp. 51–58.

Grof, S. (1998), *The Cosmic Game. Explorations of the Frontiers of Human Consciousness*. State University of New York Press, Albany.

Lozano, J.M. and Ribera, R. (2004), "A New Chance for Management, A New Challenge for Spirituality" in L. Zsolnai (Ed): *Spirituality and Ethics in Management*. Kluwer Academic Publishers. Boston, Dordrecht & London. pp. 175–185.

Pruzan, P. (2004), "Spirituality as the Context for Leadership" in L. Zsolnai (Ed): *Spirituality and Ethics in Management*. Kluwer Academic Publishers. Boston, Dordrecht & London. pp. 15–31.

Zohar, D. (2002), "Leadership Physicist" in T. Brown et al. (Eds): *Business Minds*. Financial Times – Prentice Hall, London, New York. pp. 302–307.

CHAPTER 7

Future of Capitalism*

The moral foundation of capitalism should be reconsidered. Modern capitalism is disembedded from the social and cultural norms of society and produced a deep financial, ecological and social crisis. Competitiveness is the prevailing ideology of today's business and economic policy. Companies, regions, and national economies seek to improve their productivity and gain competitive advantage. But these efforts often produce negative effects on various stakeholders at home and abroad.

The economic teachings of world religions challenge the way capitalism is functioning, and their corresponding perspectives are worthy of consideration. They represent life-serving modes of economizing which can assure the livelihood of human communities and the sustainability of natural ecosystems. Ethics and the future of capitalism are strongly connected. If we want to sustain capitalism for a long time we have to create a less violent, more caring form of it.

1 The Legitimacy of Capitalism

The financial, ecological, social crisis of the first decade of 21st century clearly show that the *legitimacy of capitalism* is in many respect questionable. The *moral foundations* of *capitalism* should be reconsidered.

---

* First published: "Future of Capitalism" in L. Zsolnai (Ed.) (2013), *Handbook of Business Ethics – Ethics in the New Economy*. Peter Lang, Oxford, Bern & Berlin. pp. 249–264.

The economic crisis of 2008–2010 produced *financial losses* of billions of USD in the form of poisoned debts, decline of stock prices and value depreciation of properties. Formerly successful economies such as Ireland, Spain, Singapore and Taiwan experienced 5–10% decline in their GDP. The fundamental cause of the crisis is the *avarice* of *consumers* fueled by *greedy financial institutions*. The prospect of future economic growth supposed to be the guarantor of the indebtedness of households, companies and economies. Today we experience the considerable downscaling of our economic activities.

Current data shows that *climate change* is more drastic in speed and magnitude than predicted. The increase of global temperature and the see level rise can be much higher because of the reactions of the degraded biosphere. The accumulated CO_2 in the atmosphere will cause devastating effects even if we would stop CO_2 emission completely today. According to James Lovelock climate change will effect tragically the humankind already by 2020 but for 2100 the majority of humankind – even 5–6 billion people – can perish because of the uncontrollable climate and the melting ice (Lovelock 2009).

According to the Millennium Ecosystem Assessment (2005), 15 out of 24 of the *ecosystem services* have been *degraded* or used unsustainably, including fresh water, capture fisheries, air and water purification, and the regulation of regional and local climate, natural hazards, and pests. These services are fundamental for the well-being of current and future human generations, and other living species. In many cases, ecosystem services have been depleted because of interventions aimed at increasing the supply of other services, such as food.

The data provided by the Living Planet Report 2008, indicate that humanity's *ecological footprint*, our impact on the Earth, has more than doubled since 1961. Since the late 1980s, mankind has been operating in overshoot. As of 2005, the Ecological Footprint has exceeded the world's biocapacity by about 30 percent. This means that the planet's resources are being used faster than they can be renewed. In parallel, the Living Planet Index shows a related and continuing loss of biodiversity (WWF International 2008).

In 2009, worldwide, 1.02 billion people were classified as *undernourished*. This represents the greatest number of hungry people since 1970 and a worsening of the unbearable trends that had emerged even before the economic crisis. In 2006–2008 a food crisis, which especially affected populations in developing countries, was created by a strong increase in international food commodity prices resulting also from international financial speculation. Because of that, at the end of 2008, domestic staple food prices remained, on average, 17 percent higher in real terms than two years earlier (FAO 2009).

Most (if not all) of the *Millennium Development Goals* (MDGs) will not be achieved by 2015. Adopted by the world leaders on 8 September 2000, thanks to the approval of the Millennium Declaration by the General Assembly of the United Nations, the MDGs concern social justice; improvements in the living conditions of children and women, particularly in developing countries; the protection of the environment; and the strengthening of international collaboration (United Nations 2009).

According to the *Happy Planet Index* (HPI) report, no country in the world is able to achieve, all at once, the three goals of high life satisfaction, high life expectancy and one-planet living. In addition, the elaborated estimates show that between 1961 and 2005 developed nations became substantially less efficient in supporting well-being (NEF 2009: 36–37).

One of the most successful capitalists of our age, *George Soros* calls the underlying ideology of global capitalism '*market fundamentalism*'. According to market fundamentalism, all kinds of values can be reduced to market values, and the free market is the only efficient mechanism that can provide for a rational allocation of resources (Soros 1998).

The market as an evaluation mechanism has inherent deficiencies. First of all, there are stakeholders that are simply non-represented in determining market values. Natural beings and future generations do not have the opportunity to vote on the marketplace. Secondly, the preferences of human individuals count rather unequally; that is, in proportion to their purchasing power, the interests of the poor and disadvantaged are necessarily underrepresented in free market settings. Thirdly, the actual preferences of the market players are rather myopic; that is, the economic agents' own interests are often misrepresented.

These inherent deficiencies imply that free markets cannot produce socially optimal outcomes. In many cases *market evaluation* is misleading from either a social or environmental point of view. This means that market is *not* a *sufficient form* of evaluating economic activities.

In its present form capitalism does need counter-veiling forces. Both politics and civil society should play important roles in correcting the deficiencies of market fundamentalism. The instabilities and inequalities of the global capitalist system could feed into nationalistic, ethnic and religious fundamentalism. In order to prevent a return to that kind of fundamentalism, we should correct the excesses of laissez faire capitalism.

2 Competitiveness and its Failures

Competitiveness is the prevailing ideology of today's business and economic policy. Companies, regions, and national economies seek to improve their productivity and gain competitive advantage. But these efforts often produce negative effects on various stakeholders at home and abroad. Competitiveness involves self-interest and aggressivity and produces monetary results at the expense of nature, society and future generations (Tencati and Zsolnai 2010).

The late *Sumantra Ghoshal* of London Business School heavily criticized the current management ideology, including competitive strategy. He argues:

> If companies exist only because of market imperfections, then it stands to reason that they would prosper by making markets as imperfect as possible. This is precisely the foundation of Porter's theory of strategy that focuses on how companies can build market power, i.e., imperfections, by developing power over their customers and suppliers, by creating barriers to entry and substitution, and by managing the interactions with their competitors. It is market power that allows a company to appropriate value for itself and prevent others from doing so. The purpose of strategy is to enhance this value-appropriating power of a company ... (Ghoshal 2005: 15).

Economic efficiency has become the greatest source of social legitimacy for business today. The focus on efficiency allows economics to neatly side-step the moral questions on what goals and whose interests any particular efficiency serves. Ghoshal refers to Nobel-laureate institutional economist *Douglas North*, who demonstrated that there is no absolute definition of efficiency. What is efficient depends on the initial distribution of rights and obligations. If that distribution changes then a different efficient solution emerges. As long as the transaction costs are positive and large, there is no way to define an efficient solution with any real meaning. And the transaction costs are not only positive and large but they are growing in our economically advanced societies (Ghoshal 2005: 24).

Competition cannot tackle the challenges generated by an unleashed globalization enabled by privatization, deregulation and liberalization (Worldwatch Institute 2006):

- the growing poverty and socioeconomic inequalities within and between nations;
- the delinking process between the richest and the poorest people/countries;
- the rise of an international criminal economy;
- the declining role of the state as a founding political institution and the absence of a real and effective political democracy at the global level;
- the increasing pressure on and the misuse/overexploitation and pollution of global environmental commons such as water, air and land;
- the depletion of biodiversity and natural resources;
- the loss of human values, such as peace, justice, dignity, solidarity and respect, in our societies.

Competition could be a very useful tool if it supported and fostered broad and shared innovation and emulation processes. But when the only purpose of our socioeconomic systems is to engage in a Darwinian 'struggle for life' on a global scale, it results in a disruptive global war among companies, affecting also the overall well-being of regions, nations and cities.

3 World Religions and their Economic Teachings

World religions have alternative views on economic life, which have great relevance for criticizing the excesses of capitalism. The economic teachings of *Judaism*, *Catholicism*, *Buddhism* and *Taoism* will be presented. Each of them challenges the way capitalism functions in our days. Other world religions (*Hinduism*, *Islam* and *Protestantism* e.g.) have developed their own alternative economic views which are also worthy of study (Bouckaert and Zsolnai (eds) 2011).

3.1 Jewish Economic Man

Meir Tamari has reconstructed the principles of Jewish economic ethics and the main features of the 'Jewish Economic Man' (Tamari 1987, 1988).

Judaism considers the role of the *entrepreneur* as legitimate and desirable. Entrepreneurs are morally entitled to a profit in return for fulfilling their function in society. The real problem is the challenge of *wealth*. How should the Jewish Economic Man use his or her accumulated wealth? What are his or her obligations to the other members of the community, especially to the poor and disabled?

It is an axiom of Judaism that stronger and more successful members of the community have a duty to provide for those who do not share their prosperity. The Hebrew word for charity (Tzedakah) has the same root as the word for 'justice'. Jewish Economic Man should give 10–20% of his or her profit for *charity* – to aid weaker and less successful members of the community.

The central point of the Jewish Economic ethics is the insistence that one should *not cause damage* – directly, indirectly or even accidentally. As the rabbinic dictum says, "One has a benefit and other does not suffer a loss." This principle poses ecological and human constraints for economic activities. Jewish Economic Man needs to choose second- or third-best alternatives, which do not harm anybody.

In Judaism man is the pinnacle of God's creation so that everything exists for the benefit of humans. However, this imposes an obligation on men and women to hand over the world to *future generations* in a state that provides *equally well* for them.

In sum, we can say that Jewish Economic Man has two fundamental obligations. First, he or she can make profit if and only if his or her activities do not harm anybody. Second, he or she should give a portion of the generated profit for charity (see also Pava 2011).

3.2 Catholic Social Teaching

The Catholic vision of economic life is based on the *Social Teaching* of the *Church* (U.S. Bishops 1986, Mele 2011).

According to Christianity, the *human person* is sacred because he or she is the clearest reflection of God on the Earth. Human dignity comes from God, not from nationality, race, sex, economic status or any human accomplishment. Thus every economic decision and institution must be judged in light of whether it protects or undermines the *dignity* of human persons.

Catholic Social Teaching generates an interconnected web of duties, rights and priorities. First, duties are defined as love and justice. Corresponding to these duties are the human rights of every person. Finally, duties and rights entail several priorities that should guide the economic choices of individuals, communities and the nation as a whole.

Love is at the heart of Christian morality: "*Love thy neighbor as thyself.*" In the framework of contemporary decision theory this commandment can be formulated in such a way that actors should give the same weight to others' payoffs as their own.

Justice has three meanings in Catholic Social Teaching. Commutative justice calls for fairness in all agreements and exchanges between individuals and social groups. Distributive justice requires the allocation of income, wealth and power to aid persons whose basic needs are unmet. Finally, social justice implies the participation of all persons in economic and social life.

In Catholic Social Teaching human rights play a fundamental role. Not only are the well-known civil and political rights emphasized but also those concerning human welfare at large. Among these 'economic rights' are the rights to life, food, shelter, rest, medical care and basic education, because all of these are indispensable to the protection of human dignity.

The main Catholic priorities for the economy include the following:

(i)   the fulfillment of the basic needs of the poor;
(ii) increased participation of excluded and vulnerable people in economic life;
(iii) the direction of investments toward the benefit of those who are poor or economically insecure;
(iv) economic and social policies to protect the strength and stability of families.

All persons are called on to contribute to the common good by seeking excellence in production and service. The freedom of business is protected but accountability of business to the common good and justice must be assured. Government has an essential moral function: protecting human rights and securing justice for all members of society.

In sum, we can say that Catholic Social Teaching favors serving the dignity of human persons. Economic activities are subordinated to this goal.

3.3 Buddhist Economics

Buddhist economics is based on the Buddhist way of life. The main goal of a Buddhist life is *liberation* from all suffering. *Nirvana* is the final state, which can be approached by want negation and purification of human character.

E.F. Schumacher described Buddhist economics in his best-selling book "Small Is Beautiful." (Schumacher, E.F. 1973).

Central values of Buddhist economics are *simplicity* and *non-violence*. From a Buddhist point of view the optimal pattern of consumption is to reach a high level of human satisfaction by means of a low rate of material consumption. This allows people to live without pressure and strain and to fulfill the primary injunction of Buddhism: "Cease to do evil; try to do good." As natural resources are limited everywhere, people living simple lifestyles are obviously less likely to be at each other's throats than those overly dependent on scarce natural resources.

According to Buddhist economics, production using local resources for local needs is the most rational way of organizing economic life. Dependence on imports from afar and the consequent need for export production is uneconomic and justifiable only in exceptional cases.

For Buddhists there is an essential difference between renewable and non-renewable resources. Non-renewable resources must be used only if they are absolutely indispensable, and then only with the greatest care and concern for conservation. To use non-renewable resources heedlessly or extravagantly is an act of violence. Economizing should be based on renewable resources as much as possible.

Buddhism does not accept the assumption of man's superiority to other species. Its motto could be, 'noblesse oblige'; that is, man must observe kindness and compassion towards natural creatures and be good to them in every way.

In sum, we can say that Buddhist economics represents a middle way between modern growth economy and traditional stagnation. It seeks the most appropriate path of development, the *Right Livelihood* for people (see also Zsolnai 2011).

3.4 The Taoist Economy

Taoism (and Confucianism) greatly influences the economies of Far Eastern countries. Studying the economic system of Taiwan, *Li-the Sun* described the main features of the Taoist Economy (Li-The Sun 1986).

Tao is the fundamental concept, which represents the way of *equilibrium* and *harmony* among myriad things of the Universe. Taoists believe that in the Universe two basic forces exist: yin and yang. *Yin* is the feminine principle; the yielding, co-operative force. *Yang* is the masculine principle; the active, competitive force. Yin and yang are complementary to each other. Humans need to find a balance between yin and yang forces in their own selves as well as in their societies. This results in the fulfillment of Tao.

In the Taoist economy two basic values play decisive roles, the *inner equilibrium* of individuals and *social harmony*. The former is necessary in resolving microeconomic problems while the latter is fundamental in handling macroeconomic issues.

At the microeconomic level the following yin and yang pairs are balanced in the Taoist economy:

(i)   public interest versus self-interest;
(ii) morality versus profit;
(iii) want negation versus want satisfaction;
(iv) cooperation versus competition;
(v)   leisure versus work.

In the Taoist economy economic activities are directed not only by self-interest. Entrepreneurs should promote the supply of public goods, and services too. Profit cannot be the sole incentive of work and investment. Since profit comes from society, a portion of it should be returned to society in the form of social responsibility. The Taoist consumer is a want regulator even without income constraints. Want negation is valued. The maximization of wants is unwise and has detrimental effects on the community and the natural environment. In production the cooperative and competitive instincts are balanced. Competition without cooperation would create chaos, but cooperation without competition would generate poverty. For people, leisure and work have equal importance. Work produces wealth while leisure is necessary for moral development.

At the macroeconomic *level* the following yin and yang pairs are balanced in the Taoist economy:

(i)   the poor versus the rich;
(ii) labor versus capital;
(iii) public sector versus private sector;
(iv) planning system versus market system;

(v) stagnation versus growth;

(vi) full employment versus price stability.

Balance between the poor and the rich requires equitable distribution of income and wealth. Taoist social policy aims at the elimination of artificial inequalities among people but does not try to eliminate natural inequalities altogether. Balance between labor and capital has two faces: one is the right proportion between labor production and machine production, and the other is the right proportion between labor ownership and capital ownership. Balance between the public sector and the private sector is necessary because the public sector provides public goods and services while the private sector assures economic efficiency. Balance between the planning system and the market system is also important, for similar reasons. Balance between stagnation and growth requires some reduction of the natural growth rate of the economy. In the Taoist economy there is no trade-off between unemployment and inflation. Since yin and yang forces rule the economy, a balance between employment and price stability is feasible.

In sum, we can say that the Taoist economy is based on the balance of yin and yang forces and tries to actualize the inner equilibrium of individuals as well as social harmony (see also Allinson 2011).

Table 1 summarizes the different responses of the studied world religions to the economic problematic.

Table 1 *World Religions and the Economic Problem*

	Basic Values	Economic Means
Judaism	causing no harm, solidarity	constraints on profit making, charity
Catholicism	love, justice	personal excellence, responsible enterprises, duties of the government
Buddhism	simplicity, non-violence	reduced consumption, using local resources, ecological conservation
Taoism	inner equilibrium of the individual, social harmony	yin & yang forces at micro-economic and macro-economic levels

4 Conclusion

Ethics and the future of capitalism are strongly connected. If we want to sustain capitalism for a long time we have to create a less violent, more caring form of it. World religions represent *life-serving modes* of *economizing* which may assure the livelihood of human communities and the sustainability of natural ecosystems. They call for a radical transformation of business. The future of capitalism is highly dependent on its ability to adapt to contemporary ecological and social reality.

References

Allinson, R. (2011), "Confucianism and Taoism" in L. Bouckaert and L. Zsolnai (Eds) 2011: *The Palgrave Handbook of Spirituality and Business*. 2011. Palgrave – Macmillan. pp. 95–102.

Bouckaert, L. and Zsolnai, L. (Eds) (2011), *The Palgrave Handbook of Spirituality and Business*. 2011. Palgrave – Macmillan.

FAO (2009), *The State of Food Insecurity in the World 2009. Economic Crises – Impacts and Lessons*. Rome.

Ghoshal, S. (2005), *Sumantra Ghoshal on Management* (Edited by Julian Birkinshaw and Gita Piramal). Prentice Hall, Harlow.

Li-teh Sun (1986), "Confucianism and the Economic Order of Taiwan" *International Journal of Social Economics* 1986(6).

Lovelock, J. (2007), "The Prophet of Climate Change: James Lovelock" *Rolling Stone Magazine* Oct 17.

Mele, D. (2011), "Catholic Social Teaching" in L. Bouckaert and L. Zsolnai (Eds) 2011: *The Palgrave Handbook of Spirituality and Business*. 2011. Palgrave – Macmillan. pp. 118–128.

Millennium Ecosystem Assessment (2005), *Ecosystems and Human Well-being: Synthesis* Island Press, Washington, DC.

NEF (2009), *The Happy Planet Index 2.0. Why Good Lives Don't Have to Cost the Earth*, The New Economics Foundation, London.

Pava, M. (2011), "Jewish Economic Perspective on Income and Wealth Distribution" in L. Bouckaert and L. Zsolnai (Eds) 2011: *The Palgrave Handbook of Spirituality and Business*. 2011. Palgrave – Macmillan. pp. 111–117.

Schumacher, E.F. (1973), *Small is beautiful*. 1973. Abacus, London.

Soros, G. (1988), *The Crisis of Global Capitalism*. 1998. Little, Brown and Company, London.

Tamari, M. (1987), *With All Your Possessions: Jewish Ethics and Economic Life*. 1987. The Free Press, New York.

Tamari, M. (1988), *The Social Responsibility of the Corporation: a Jewish Perspective*. 1988. Bank of Israel.

Tencati, A. and Zsolnai, L. (2009), "The Collaborative Enterprise" *Journal of Business Ethics*. 2009, 85 (3), pp. 367–376.

United Nations (2009), *The Millennium Development Goals Report 2009*. United Nations Department of Economic and Social Affairs, New York, NY.

U.S. Bishops (1986), "Economic Justice for All" *Origins* 1986, 24.

Worldwatch Institute (2006), *State of the World 2006. The Challenge of Global Sustainability*. Earthscan, London.

WWF International (2008), *Living Planet Report 2008*.

Zsolnai, L. (ed) (2011), *Ethical Principles and Economic Transformation: A Buddhist Approach*. Springer.

CHAPTER 8

Why Frugality?*

In the international colloquium "Does Frugality Make Sense?" held in Leuven in 2002, *Philippe Van Parijs* summed up six hypotheses as to why frugality might be relevant in today's context. Frugal tastes facilitate happiness, and they create the conditions for concerns about justice. Frugal habits constitute a personal asset, allow a Pareto improvement, are required for a fair distribution of resources, and are perhaps intrinsically better.

1 The Frugality Project

Frugality and the complex interplay between spirituality and economic rationality formed the core of our research project "Spirituality and the Economics of Frugality." This project was proposed by *Luk Bouckaert* (K.U. Leuven), *Hendrik Opdebeeck* (University of Antwerp), *Luc Van Liedekerke* (K.U. Leuven & University of Antwerp) and *Laszlo Zsolnai* (Corvinus University of Budapest). It was launched as the research program of the European SPES Forum, which is an international network promoting Spirituality in Economics and Society (http://www.eurospes.be).

The aims of the Frugality project were threefold. The first aim was to clarify the concept of frugality as a form of spiritual capital. The intention was not only to create an overview of the different spiritual approaches to

*   First published: "Why Frugality?" in L. Bouckaert, H. Opdebeeck and L. Zsolnai (Eds) (2008), *Frugality: Rebalancing Material and Spiritual Values in Economic Life.* Peter Lang, Oxford. pp. 3–23. (Co-authors: *Luk Bouckaert* and *Hendrik Opdebeeck*).

frugality in Buddhist, Christian, Jewish, Islamic and philosophical traditions, but also to tackle the pitfall of instrumentalization. Is it possible to
transform the spiritual meanings of frugality into economic (instrumental)
categories such as 'capital', 'investment' and 'utility maximization' without losing their intrinsic motivation? How can frugality be expressed as a
spiritual concern *in* economic and business life? The general assumption
is that, although frugality is contrary to consumerism and wild economic
growth, it is not contrary to economic rationality as such. It challenges
economic theories to introduce nonmaterial and noninstrumental values
in the framework of economic decision making and in the models of preference maximization.

Second, research was worked out to explore on a theoretical basis
the socioeconomic consequences of the practice of frugality. Related to
the interest and backgrounds of the investigators, the project explores the
following consequences: (1) The consequences of frugality for organizational and managerial ethics. (2) The consequences of frugality for welfare
policies. This requires a public-goods approach to frugality based on the
analysis of external effects and Pareto improvement; e.g., the arguments of
Robert Frank for a progressive consumption tax on luxury goods. (3) The
consequences of frugality for global sustainability and intergenerational
justice. The notion of sustainability has reintroduced the idea of limits
within the spheres of business, consumption and global policies. But the
cost of sustainability must be distributed in a fair way between rich and
poor countries and between generations. The project explores how frugality as a global good is a necessary condition for global sustainability and
intergenerational justice.

Finally, central to the project was a set of case studies in business where
entrepreneurs developed strategies to find a reflective equilibrium between
spiritual and material aspirations. These strategies are linked to the style
of leadership, the acceptance of limits in growth, the relation to clients
and the use of profit.

We define frugality as an ideal and an *art de vivre*, which implies low
material consumption and a simple lifestyle, to open the mind for spiritual goods as inner freedom, social peace and justice or the quest for God
or 'ultimate reality'. Frugality as a conception of the good life has deep

philosophical and religious roots in the East and the West. Monks and religious people all over the world practice it in different forms of asceticism, self-restriction or free-chosen poverty ('voluntary simplicity'). But even nonreligious philosophers in the tradition of Epicurean ethics or the Stoa emphasize that frugal tastes and lasting enjoyment go hand in hand. Although for religious ethics frugality is a spiritual virtue, for nonreligious ethics it is a rational virtue to enhance happiness.

In economics, the frugal and industrious man has been praised by Adam Smith and promoted by Max Weber as the embodiment of worldly asceticism, the protestant driver of early capitalism. But by focusing on the instrumental value of frugality as a means to increase material welfare, they initiated a shift in the meaning of frugality. Frugality became related to savings and to investments for enhancing future welfare. This instrumentalization of frugality ends paradoxically in its elimination on the economic scene. Consumerism and material greed, just the opposite of frugality, are the basic drivers for increasing wealth and lead to an erosion of the intrinsic and spiritual meaning of frugality.

This paper aims to answer the following questions: What arguments do we have for reintroducing frugality to economic life? What are the spiritual resources that foster a frugal lifestyle? What are the social and economic implications on a macro and micro level? How can we connect frugality to more accepted ideas such as sustainability in business, ethical consumption or distributive justice? What kinds of practices can realize and promote frugality today?

2 Issues of Frugality

We here summarize the main points developed by the participants of the Frugality project.

In his paper "Rational versus Spiritual Concept of Frugality," *Luk Bouckaert* (Catholic University of Leuven and European SPES Forum) argues for the shift from a rational to a spiritual concept of frugality in social ethics and business practices (Bouckaert 2008).

Bouckaert begins his analysis with the rational philosophy of Epicurus. The *Epicurean ethics* of sustainable enjoyment provides us with two principles about frugality. The first principle states that frugality is the result of a rational assessment of pains and pleasures. We may not know clearly what pleasure is, but we do know pain, anxiety and confusion, so we can continue to seek pleasure by banishing all forms of pain, anxiety and confusion. The highest form of pleasure is 'ataraxia' – or imperturbability – a state in which the soul is as the sea when the wind has calmed. The second principle of Epicurus is to simplify our needs. The more desires one has, the greater the chance that they will not be satisfied, thus leading to suffering. So a person ought to restrict and simplify his or her needs.

Frugality, as Epicurus taught us, is a rational virtue. Activities and needs should be ordered in such a way as to lead to maximal pleasure in the long term and a proper balance among the various sorts of needs. Sustainability in today's business world has a similar logic. Business sustainability seeks a proper balance among financial, social and ecological objectives and, in the name of future generations, puts limits to our welfare ambitions. But short-term pressures of the market may lead to quite the opposite of long-term social and ecological value creation. Despite its ethical attractiveness and social necessity, sustainable business practice seems doomed to failure, notwithstanding all rational arguments to the contrary.

Although the 'Spiritual Homo economicus' does not exist in textbooks of mainstream economics, he or she might be found among entrepreneurs and business leaders, whether they are for-profit or social-profit organizations. His or her profile would comprise one who is market-oriented, efficient and driven by a genuine social and ecological spirituality.

For Bouckaert the famous painting St. John the Baptist in the Wilderness by Geertgen tot Sint Jans represents an illuminating example of *spiritual frugality*. Spiritual frugality releases the human mind from the active, self-seeking ego. By this move from ego-centeredness to other-centeredness the world is transformed from a wilderness into a garden, similar to the biblical Garden of Eden. This spiritual interpretation of frugality has another intentional and motivational structure than the rational, Epicurean approach or the ascetic approach of some religious traditions.

For Epicurus, the cause of our inability to enjoy lies in the short-sightedness of reason: People seek short-time gain rather than durable and lasting satisfactions; they chase after all manner of imagined or inculcated needs at the expense of basic human needs. For St. John, the source of our inability to experience the joy of life is of a different order: Human reason is blinded because it takes the logic of self-interest as the ultimate standard. It is no longer capable of listening to the voice of the invisible Other or hearing the inner voice of things. These two perspectives give rise to a permanent tension between spirituality and rationality. One can, for example, undertake all sorts of charitable works or ascetic exercises with the perhaps-unconscious goal of enhancing one's ego rather than listening to the Other – an ambiguity to which many spiritual writers draw our attention.

The same ambiguity can also be found in sustainable business practice. The contemporary practice of dealing prudently and frugally with the environment uses arguments that are mostly based on a standpoint of well-considered self-interest and long-term benefit. But here, too, the practice of sustainability will only succeed if it is supported by a sense of ecological interconnectedness.

By presenting the case of the *Trappist Brewery of Westmalle* in Belgium, Bouckaert provides an inspiring example of how a spiritual concept of frugality can be combined with good entrepreneurship. At present it is a private limited company that belongs to the monks of the Trappist Abbey of Westmalle. Under the monks' supervision the modern brewery is managed by a team of competent laypeople and their beer is consistently awarded among the best in the world. Although the company is highly modernized and successful in its commercial activities, the balance between spiritual and material needs is part of the production and distribution process. The spirit of frugality is implemented in concrete choices about the quality of the product, the scale of the production, the relations with the personnel, the advertisement, and the use of profit. It is clear that the business decisions are not commanded by the logic of maximizing income and financial profit for the Abbey. They have a spiritual bottom line expressed in the charter of the brewery. The key elements of this charter are (i) limits to growth,

(ii) deep ecological respect, (iii) work as a spiritual value, (iv) honest and sober advertisement and (v) sharing profit.

Spiritual-based enterprises are different in size, production factors, and religious convictions but we always found the same ingredients of frugality praxis in them as in the Trappist Abbey of Westmalle. For some entrepreneurs it remains difficult to see the difference between the ethical/rational and the spiritual approach. Bouckaert reassures us that although there is a rational case for a spiritual and frugal life, the meaning of a frugal and spiritual life cannot be fully expressed in rational terms. It requires an immediate awareness of the nonfunctional, intrinsic or symbolic presence of things. A genuine spirituality of frugality needs instrumental economic rationality to implement it but cannot be substituted by rational economics. What we need is a *spiritual-based* and *rationally implemented* praxis of frugality (Bouckaert 2008).

In his paper "Frugality and the Body," Cambridge-based missioner and priest *Rafael Esteban* explores the theories of Chilean economist Manfred Max-Neef on "human needs and satisfiers" to set the foundation for a critique of the dominant economics of growth, which leads not only to unsustainable consumption and lack of distributive justice but to a radical debasement of human beings as "material consumers" with the loss of their spiritual worth as 'temples of the Holy Spirit' (Esteban 2008).

Esteban criticizes the dominant development paradigm, which sees communities and people of the Third World as undeveloped and undermines their well-integrated traditional settings and cultural structures. This is caused by the blindness of the agents of change to the cultural values and wealth of those communities. Coming from the rich world, we have related to them as poor beggars, and that is what they have become. It is a clear case of a self-fulfilling prophecy. This is the result of asymmetrically destructive power relations in which our economist ideology, by reducing all needs to material needs, makes us blind to spiritual values and strips people of dignity while feeding them.

The ideology of the consumer culture promises happiness in the acquisition and consumption of an ever-increasing amount of commodities, but the economic system built on it does not satisfy real needs. On the contrary, it creates ever-increasing wants by cultivating greed and results in structural dissatisfaction. The obsession with the satisfaction of material wants slides in a frantic grab for luxury. This relates fully to the fornication against which St. Paul warns us: our prostitution to Mammon.

Max-Neef's economic theory aims at rethinking the modern Western notions of poverty and wealth with a systemic understanding of human nature (Max Neef 1991, 1992, 1998). For Max-Neef, human nature is defined by a system of human needs that have to be satisfied throughout life to result in human growth. Material (bodily) needs are but a small part of the system of basic needs. There are nine human needs altogether: subsistence, protection, affection, understanding, participation, creation, recreation, identity and freedom. These human needs have to be satisfied at the four existential modes as follows: being, having, doing and interacting. When the nine needs are combined with the four existential modes, this produces a matrix of 36 cells, which can be filled with a complex system of satisfiers.

Esteban states that Max-Neef's distinction between needs and satisfiers and the shift in reflection from material poverty exclusively to a plurality of poverties have proven to be first class tools for assessing the health of individuals and groups (families, communities, organizations, cultures). A systemic approach highlights the connection among (i) human needs, (ii) human rights as comprised by the right of all to access to a harmonic system of satisfiers of human needs and (iii) the responsibility of all (individuals and groups) to contribute in the measure of their potential to the health of the system.

In Max-Neef's perspective societies and individuals can be dysfunctional not only through deprivation of the economic goods but also through the excess consumption of those same goods. The world is not divided between the 'haves' and the 'have-nots' but between a majority that do not have enough and a minority that has too much. And the real trouble is that the deprived majority does not aspire to have enough for a decent human living but aspires to participate in the unlimited race to growth of the consumer society, deepening the unsustainability of the present economic system.

The strategies for real human development have to be based, not on increased production and consumption of economic goods, but on the creation and nurturing of synergistic satisfiers propped by a minimum of economic goods. *Frugality* enters the picture here as the ability to find what is the essential use of material resources and economic goods needed to achieve the satisfaction of all basic needs in a given situation. This puts economic goods ('the body') in their right place at the service of 'healthy (holy) living' and interacting: the body becomes the temple of the spirit.

To propose an alternative economic system based on frugality, Esteban uses the example of Basic Christian Communities in Central and Latin America. *Basic Christian Communities* (BSCs) are constituted from a complex system of noneconomic inputs and need little in the shape of economic resource infrastructure. They rely on what is locally available and keep infrastructures to a minimum, preferring to use local resources to tackle challenges in their social environment. This is needed to remain autonomous and insure self-reliance. BCCs are small and local and do not need complex (and expensive) administrative or physical structures.

Esteban suggests that it is not evident that we should find inspiration from the main world religions (Christianity, Islam, Hinduism and Buddhism) to develop an alternative paradigm to consumerism. It is perhaps in the spiritual wealth and experience of the rich variety of ethnic religions that we can find precious patterns of how to be human. The most interesting thing is that BCCs try to recover the best of what is lost through the progressive disintegration of traditional cultures. Autonomous communities – through a great adaptation to the possibilities of their environment – create sustainable ways of life that respect the rules of life itself and provide ways toward human flourishing for the greatest number. Following the examples of survival cultures, we have to develop a culture and an economy that prizes nonmaterial goods (the spirit) above material goods (the body). An economy that gives priority to synergistic satisfiers of nonmaterial needs could grow without squandering our limited material resources. We have to abandon the 'idolatry of the body' if we want to survive and flourish as human beings without destroying the world (Esteban 2008).

In his paper "How the Idea 'Created Co-Creator' Can Contribute to the Nurturing of Frugality in Economic Life," *Francis Kadaplackal* (Catholic University of Leuven) argues that the theological concept 'created co-creator' can be a good tool for conceptualizing the concept of frugality and can thus contribute to the shaping of attitudes and behaviors favorable to sustainability, environmental protection and ethically qualified consumption (Kadaplackal 2008).

The term *'created co-creator'* was introduced by *Philip Hefner* (1988, 1993, 1997, 2004). According to Hefner, human beings are God's created co-creators whose purpose is to be the agency, acting in freedom, to birth the future that is most wholesome for the nature that has birthed us – the nature that is not only our own genetic heritage, but also the entire human community and the evolutionary and ecological reality to which we belong. Exercising this agency is said to be God's will for humans.

Kapdalackal argues that the theology of the created co-creator offers us an ethically justifiable and theologically qualified anthropological framework, which can help us to reaffirm and reposition frugality in the modern world. The growth of consumerism and the impacts of globalization have continually downplayed the meaning, function and significance of frugality. But the concept created co-creator can open up new possibilities to place it back on track.

First, the theology of the created co-creator reiterates that the human person has to be perceived as a creature, created by God in love. The fact that we are created explains our dependency on God, nature and other human beings for our existence. Our role and function in the world cannot be understood in terms of separate entities, but are instead incorporated into the purposes of creation. As creatures, we are not above the natural world, but we are part of it. The created co-creator posits respect for nature as an essential condition and as a basic attitude that should characterize our life on earth. If we truly respect the natural world, we should accept the limits that are imposed on us by nature and embrace a frugal way of life.

Second, that we are created refers also to our relationality. It is through a spectrum of relationships that the human person realizes his or her human dignity, which flows forth from the dignity of God. In our interactions with the natural world and other human beings, we are called upon to foster respect, love, concern, and care for all that God has created. The relational dimension also invites us to foster sharing as an important element of our life. Frugality can help us overcome our selfishness and egoism, which result in the abuse of the resources of the earth. Moderation gains ethical qualification through the limited use of the earth's resources, but it gains even more when it operates by fostering the willingness to share what we have with others.

Third, freedom can be considered the defining category of the created co-creator. Freedom presupposes responsibility as a necessary condition. Acting in freedom, the created co-creator has to make choices in life that are in line with the purposes of creation. As a choice frugality can be justified because it helps create a just society by eradicating social and economic inequalities that have deep roots in contemporary societies. A frugal lifestyle can help the just and equitable distribution of the earth's goods. As Mahatma Gandhi used to say, "There is enough for everyone's need, but not for everyone's greed."

Fourth, the created co-creator stresses the creative qualities of the human person. We are called upon to be creative in our life so that we can continue the creative work of God and bring the creation to the purposes that God has for it. A frugal way of life involves an active engagement to develop the world and the natural resources in the best possible way. Frugality can help us to make those choices that are not detrimental to the environment. Through hard work the created co-creator brings creation to its perfection and defends the proper use of material goods through the practice of temperance.

Fifth, the creative dimension of the human person can also help us to highlight the necessity to build up a *sustainable society*. Creativity involves the prudent and sustainable use of nature and natural resources. We are responsible not only for the present state of affairs, but also for the future of the world. Genuine development should take into account the rights of *future generations* to a habitable place. As created co-creators we are responsible for leaving behind a healthy environment for those yet to come. Frugality enables us to extend our concern not only to the world as it exists, but also to future generations (Kadaplackal 2008).

In his paper "Quaker Simplicity" Oxford-based environmentalist *Laurie Michaelis* analyzes simplicity in the *Quaker tradition*. Quakers have practiced an ethic of simplicity since their 17th-century origins. For much of the 20th century that ethic kept a low profile in Friends' identity and discourse. But it is a shared core value for all Quaker groups. Liberal Quakers are paying renewed attention to *simplicity* concerning the environmental and social impacts of the Western lifestyle (Michaelis 2008).

A commitment to simplicity had several functions for earlier Quakers. First, it was seen as a condition for a healthy relationship with God and the self and a central virtue for the Christian life. Second, it was an aspect of a healthy relationship with others in an egalitarian community within a society where old hierarchies would be abolished. Third, it was a condition for a healthy relationship with the wider sphere of humans and other life forms.

The Quaker ethic of simplicity has developed throughout the centuries. Its prominent values and characteristics include the following: (i) commitment to freedom of individual thoughts and beliefs, with respect and encouragement given for the ideas, insights and concerns of individuals; (ii) pluralism in theology and personal spiritual paths; (iii) an egalitarian and inclusive framework where anyone present may speak both in meetings for worship and in meetings for administration and decision making; (iv) encouragement for selflessness – individuals are expected to lay aside their own positions and interests in such meetings; (v) strong concern for due process; (vi) repeated and careful testing of decisions in a hierarchy of meetings, starting with the individual in the local meeting and working up to the national level in the Yearly Meeting; and (vii) extensive allocation of roles within the structure but always for limited periods so that individuals do not become attached to their positions.

In 2002, a network of Quaker meetings (coordinated by Michaelis) set to work in the *Living Witness Project*, exploring and developing approaches to sustainable living in groups. The project is essentially an action inquiry, encouraging participating groups to experiment with diverse approaches and to reflect and learn together from the outcomes. While some groups have focused on encouraging participants to change their own lifestyles, the most successful groups are those that have developed a range of outward-looking activities. Participants in those groups do report changes to simplify their own lifestyles or to adopt environmentally friendly technology. These changes seem to happen as a result of being part of a group with shared and articulated values, augmented by a tendency toward congruence of those articulated values with lifestyles and actions. Some individuals in these groups have developed low-impact lifestyles, generating less than 5 percent of the UK average of waste per person (after recycling and composting), and producing less than 20 percent of the UK average of greenhouse gas emissions. They have found that lifestyle change is possible, that it is much easier with the support of an ongoing group, and that it can be a fascinating and joyful experience.

Quaker approaches may be accessible to secular groups partly because Quakers stress processes rather than beliefs. They are of interest for individualized societies, because Quakers have found ways of balancing the diversity of individual approaches with the need to develop a community of shared values and mutual support. In the end, Michaelis argues, we should seek to learn whatever we can from a group that has shown the ability to make a conscious choice for simplicity (Michaelis 2008).

In his paper "Overconsumption" political activist and sociologist *Dirk Geldof* (of the Flemish Green Party) argues that to get broader support for frugality and sufficiency, we have to recognize the functions of consumption. It is possible to frame sufficiency and frugality as positive ways to a better quality of life. Only if we succeed in creating such a positive image and stimulating praxis can it become an alternative to the present overconsumption, which is not only unsustainable and socially unjust but causes welfare-related diseases (Geldof 2008).

Geldof believes that Western lifestyles and overconsumption are a dead end. They are not sustainable, they force people to work harder and longer, and the end result is that increased consumption no longer increases satisfaction or happiness. *Sufficiency* can be an alternative to overconsumption. First, sufficiency is a crucial element in strategies for sustainability, besides efficiency and consistency. Second, sufficiency and downshifting are alternatives to the retrace resulting from the cycle of work-and-spend. Third, sufficiency and downshifting will give us more time to enjoy our lives, rather than exacerbating tension between our endless desires and the lack of means.

But sufficiency can gain importance for larger groups of wealthy societies, if we stress the positive functions of consumption. Sufficiency should not be about saying goodbye to material wealth and repressing all our desires. We should focus on how to deal with our wealth, how to satisfy our desires more deeply and how to enjoy a qualitatively better life by consuming less. The *Slow Food Movement* is a fantastic example. It is a way toward using more qualitative foods and meals, in a more convivial society, while recognizing the ecological limits of the earth. It is a way toward greater and more intense pleasure through accepting limits (Geldof 2008).

In their paper "Frugality and the Moral Economy of Late Modern Capitalism," *Ronald Commers* and *Wim Vandekerckhove* (Ghent University) reflect on the spirits of capitalism from a historical perspective. They show that the 18th-century debate between Mandeville and Shaftesbury resonates with the different conceptualizations of stakeholder and their implications for corporate governance. They argue that the notion of frugality is important with regard to interhuman relations of production and favor the changing of public standards of taste justifying frugality's issues. They link frugality in production with frugality in consumption and give a modest defense of frugality in economic terms (Commers and Vandekerckhove 2008).

Commers and Vanderkerckhove recall that at the end of the 17th and the beginning of the 18th centuries, *Mandeville* spoke out against frugality for the few, on the condition that they could afford a good life of more or less controlled big spending. And he opposed respectable life conditions and human dignity for the paupers. The best they could hope for was a frugal life free from the harshest forms of misery. The *Earl of Shaftesbury*, by contrast, contested the benefits of luxury for all men, rich or poor. It is not that money and material wealth are in themselves harmful, but the temptations linked with them spoil the human character and civic behavior of the many. A luxurious life, by all means, will be injurious to social sensibility and the power of reasonable judgment in the individual human person. Frugality in matters of desire and simplicity in the human condition will promote and stimulate social bonds between fellow men. To this purpose they should free themselves from the desire to consume.

Commers and Vanderkerckhove show that the disagreement between Mandeville and Shaftersbury depicts one of the most crucial concepts today in business ethics – the concept of *stakeholder*. Goodpaster (1991) and Sternberg (1999) follow the Mandevillean line of reasoning: the best that workers can hope for is "a frugal life, free of the harshest form of misery." Milton Friedman's formulation is that there is a fiduciary relationship between management and shareholders and the best other stakeholders can count on are considerations of common morality (Friedman 1970). The implied corporate governance here remains centered around the principal-agent theory and the primacy of the shareholder. On the other hand Wicks, Gilbert and Freeman (1994) follow Shaftesbury's line of thinking: to maintain the coexistence of perspectives and take care of the interdependencies among various stakeholders, one needs to forgo maximization of any single stake or interest – thus engendering a frugality for all. With regard to corporate governance, this line of thinking favors democracy in the workplace and is centered around co-determination by the various stakeholders.

Commers and Vanderkerckhove insist that frugality with regard to the desire to consume must be linked with frugality in corporate governance. Thus it seems that the *new consumerism* cannot do without co-determination at the workplace. We cannot have the affluence for the few unless we disconnect and disrupt equal relationships between individuals and their embeddings in communities. Frugality urges us, Commers and Vanderkerckhove point out, to use a discourse of inclusive responsibility (Commers and Vandekerckhove 2008).

In their paper "Consumerism and Frugality – Contradictory Principles in Economics?" *Knut Ims* (Norwegian School of Economics and Business Administration, Bergen) and *Ove Jakobsen* (Bodø Graduate School of Business) argue that to attain a sustainable scale of production and consumption, fair distribution of resources and wealth, and efficient resource allocation, rethinking economy within a worldview characterized by integration, dynamics and holism must occur. They suggest that we should think of sustainability and life quality as overriding goals (Ims and Jakobsen 2008).

For Ims and Jakobsen frugality means that individuals practice restraint in both acquiring and using economic goods and services in order to achieve lasting and more fulfilling goals. At an aggregated level, frugality stresses low consumption that meets long-term personal, familial, and communal needs. Another ideal of frugality is to reduce waste by changing habits of consumption.

Ims and Jakobsen argue that in the *Aristotelian Christian tradition* we can find important, inspiring sources of an economy of frugality. In the Thomistic tradition, one important notion is that the use of external goods has a natural limit. Material wealth is needed to a certain extent, but it should be used only as an instrument. This view corresponds to Aristotle's golden mean, which in several ways can stand as a model of an economy based on frugality, because it condemns excesses.

Ims and Jakobsen find that growth in production and consumption is translated to welfare in a mechanical perspective. Growth in welfare is an important goal in most countries today. If we change the focus to frugality, we find that this concept has to have connotations for *life quality* and *well-being* (Ims and Jakobsen 2008).

In his paper "The Urgency of a Frugality-Based Economics" *Hendrik Opdebeeck* (University of Antwerp) analyzes E.F. Schumacher's contribution to a frugality-based economics. Schumacher developed an alternative, intermediary economic system for a society that is in need of stability and change, of traditions and reforms, of the protection of public and private interest, of growth and decay, and of order and freedom (Opdebeeck 2008).

The ethics of an economy that guarantees peace insists on the value of *enough*, or frugality, so that discontentment and violence against nature and man can be avoided. Schumacher says, "We must define the economic concept of 'enough.' If there is no idea of 'enough,' all problems become insoluble." The reason that the violence provoked by the economic system has not (yet) led to destroying that system is that interpersonal violence is being channeled into international problems and dangers like the explosive arms race and environmental degradation.

Opdebeeck states that a more encompassing paradigm based on frugality (involving a lower consumption) is required and doubts whether eliminating scarcity or maximizing utility are valid as relevant points of departure for our time. Rather, the case can be made that today's major problems may well in essence be caused by the central position awarded to scarcity and utility as basic categories. Thus there is a need to elaborate a *frugality-based economic paradigm* that is able to tackle contemporary problems in a less one-sided manner. Here we are back at the origins of the word frugality in Latin: *frugalis*, meaning useful in a worthy way, and *frux*, meaning productive in a fruitful way. In this way the general assumption becomes evident that while frugality is contrary to consumerism and excessive economic productivity and growth, it is not contrary to economic usefulness or rationality (Opdebeeck 2008).

In his paper "Frugality First," *Herman Daly* (University of Maryland) uses ecological-economics arguments to show that frugality should precede efficiency in achieving sustainability. He suggests understanding *sustainability* in the terms of *throughput*. According to Daly physical throughput should be sustained; that is, the entropic physical flow from nature's sources through the economy and back to nature's sink should be nondeclining (Daly 2008).

Daly states that the problem with 'efficiency first' is what comes second. An improvement in efficiency alone is equivalent to having a larger supply of the factor whose efficiency increased. The price of that factor declines and more uses for the cheaper factor are found. The net result is that there is greater consumption of the resource than before, even if it is produced more efficiently. So scale continues to grow. A policy of 'frugality first', however, induces efficiency as a secondary effect even while "efficiency first" does not induce frugality. The main task of our age is to *limit* the *scale* of the *economy* relative to the ecosystem by restraining uneconomic growth that increases costs by more than it increases benefits, thus making us poorer instead of richer (Daly 2008).

In their paper "Frugal Marketing: Can Selling Less Make Business Sense?" *Ronald Jeurissen* (Nyenrode Business University) and *Bert van de Ven* (Tilburg University) explore the intricate and paradoxical relationships between frugality and marketing. Their starting point is that marketing will in some way respond to a frugality trend. It may seem paradoxical that marketing should be able to deal with beliefs and attitudes that aim at consuming less, but frugality offers several marketing opportunities, depending on how the value and virtue of frugality are perceived and practiced by consumers (Jeurissen and van de Ven 2008).

Marketing seems hostile to frugality in at least two ways, state Jeurissen and van de Ven. First, it looks as though marketing is in conflict with the virtue of frugality. Frugality is a way for people to gain control over their lives by freeing themselves from the pressures of the consumer role and the constraints and uncertainties of being an employee. A major reason for downshifting is that people want more time, less stress and more balance in their lives. Marketing, however, seems to cultivate a hedonistic and materialistic worldview. It teaches consumers that fast gratification of needs is the norm, rather than making considered and balanced consumer choices. Second, marketing seems hostile to the goal of sustainability, which is an important motive behind the frugal lifestyle. One of the important drives of the frugality movement is the consideration that present rates of production and consumption are unsustainable.

Jeurissen and van de Ven distinguish between individual and political frugality. In individual frugality, the emphasis is on enhancing individual life-quality through reduced consumption. Downshifting consumption becomes an individual consumer choice. Political 'frugalists' believe that individual frugal choices are not enough, as they leave the political and economic organization of overproduction and overconsumption unaltered. Frugality should be based on a political economy of frugality, and it should become a political movement.

For Jeurissen and van de Ven, frugality seems only conceivable as a retreat from the world of consumption and work, through a compilation of counter-measures: doing less, consuming less and differently, increasing the number of buy-nothing days in favor of contemplation, consuming attentively, and enjoying all things that come for free or have already been paid for. Frugality as a retreat from the world can be the expression of a strong spiritual orientation in life. The core of many forms of spirituality is becoming aware of one's own awareness of being in the world. This mode of being is accessible through reflection and meditation (Jeurissen and van de Ven 2008).

In his paper "Progressive Consumption Tax," *Robert Frank* (Cornell University) asks the question of whether consuming more goods makes people happier. The large and growing scientific literature on the determinants of life-satisfaction and psychosocial well-being suggests that for a broad spectrum of goods, beyond some point the answer is essentially no. Evidence from this literature also suggests, however, that there are ways of spending time and money that do have the potential to increase

people's satisfaction with their lives, and herein lies a message of considerable importance for policymaking (Frank 2008).

Frank argues that if our problem is that some forms of private consumption seem more attractive to individuals than to society as a whole,
the simplest solution is to make those forms less attractive by taxing them.
Without raising our tax bill at all, a *progressive consumption tax* would
change our incentives in precisely the desired way.

Taxing consumption progressively, observes Frank, is different from
consumption taxes such as the value-added tax. Those types of taxes are
levied at the same rate no matter how much a family consumes. They are
regressive because wealthy families usually save much higher proportions
of their income than poor families. But the consumption tax proposed by
Frank is not regressive at all. Its escalating marginal tax rates on consumption, coupled with its large standard deduction, insure that total tax as a
proportion of income rises steadily with income, even though the assumed
savings rate is sharply higher for high-income families. If consumption
were taxed at a progressive rate, we would save more, buy less expensive
houses and cars, and feel less pressure to work excessively long hours. And
this, on the best available evidence, would *improve* the *quality* of *our lives*
(Frank 2008).

3 Conclusion

The present unsustainable lifestyle of mankind requires drastic changes.
Western-style consumer capitalism has failed. It has resulted in global climate change, dramatic ecosystem degradation and biodiversity loss. Also,
it has caused massive unhappiness and emptiness in rich countries and
social disintegration worldwide.

The interests of nature, society and future generations require a considerable reduction of material throughput of the economy and a reorienta-
tion of our economic activities. This could become possible by employing
a more spiritual approach to life and the economy.

The rational case for frugality is a limited one. By rational choice we can develop a more frugal and sufficient way of life, but material temptations can always overwrite our ecological, social and ethical considerations. But the spiritual case for frugality is strong enough. Spiritually based frugal practices may lead to rational outcomes such as reducing ecological destruction, social disintegration and the exploitation of future generations.

References

Bouckaert, L. (2008), "Rational versus Spiritual Concepts of Frugality" in L. Bouckaert, H. Opdebeeck and L. Zsolnai (Eds): *Frugality: Rebalancing Material and Spiritual Values in Economic Life*. 2008. Peter Lang, Oxford. pp. 27–44.

Commers, R. and Vandekerckhove, W. (2008), "Frugality and Moral Economy of Late Modern Capitalism" in L. Bouckaert, H. Opdebeeck and L. Zsolnai (Eds): *Frugality: Rebalancing Material and Spiritual Values in Economic Life*. 2008. Peter Lang, Oxford. pp. 141–168.

Daly, H. (2008), "Frugality First" in L. Bouckaert, H. Opdebeeck and L. Zsolnai (Eds): *Frugality: Rebalancing Material and Spiritual Values in Economic Life*. 2008. Peter Lang, Oxford. pp. 207–226.

Esteban, R. (2008), "Frugality and the Body" in L. Bouckaert, H. Opdebeeck and L. Zsolnai (Eds): *Frugality: Rebalancing Material and Spiritual Values in Economic Life*. 2008. Peter Lang, Oxford. pp. 45–70.

Frank, R. (2004), "Can Socially Responsible Firms Survive in Competitive Environments?" in R. Frank: *What Price the Moral High Ground? Ethical Dilemmas in Competitive Environments*. 2004. Princeton University Press, Princeton and Oxford.

Frank, R. (2008), "The Progressive Consumption Tax" in L. Bouckaert, H. Opdebeeck and L. Zsolnai (Eds): *Frugality: Rebalancing Material and Spiritual Values in Economic Life*. 2008. Peter Lang, Oxford. pp. 249–278.

Friedman, M. (1970), "The Social Responsibility of Business Is to Increase its Profits," *New York Times Magazine* 13 September 1970.

Geldof, D. (2008), "Overconsumption" in L. Bouckaert, H. Opdebeeck and L. Zsolnai (Eds): *Frugality: Rebalancing Material and Spiritual Values in Economic Life*. 2008. Peter Lang, Oxford. pp. 125–140.

Goodpaster, K.E. (1991), "Business Ethics and Stakeholder Analysis," *Business Ethics Quarterly* vol. 1, no. 1, pp. 53–73.

Hefner, P. (1988), "The Evolution of the Created Co-Creator," *Currents in Theology and Mission*, Vol. 15, 1988 December, pp. 512–525.

Hefner, P. (1993), *The Human Factor. Evolution, Culture and Religion*. Fortress Press, Minneapolis.

Hefner, P. (1997), "Biocultural Evolution of the Created Co-Creator," *Dialog*, Vol. 36, 1997 Summer, pp. 197–205.

Hefner, P. (2004), "Editorial. Human Being: Questioning and Being Questioned," *Zygon*, Vol. 39, 2004 December, pp. 733–735.

Ims, K. and Jakobsen, O. (2008), "Consumerism and Frugality: Contradictory Principles in Economics?" in L. Bouckaert, H. Opdebeeck and L. Zsolnai (Eds): *Frugality: Rebalancing Material and Spiritual Values in Economic Life*. 2008. Peter Lang, Oxford. pp. 169–184.

Jeurissen, R. and van de Ven, B. (2008), "Frugal Marketing: Can Selling Less Make Business Sence?" in L. Bouckaert, H. Opdebeeck and L. Zsolnai (Eds): *Frugality: Rebalancing Material and Spiritual Values in Economic Life*. 2008. Peter Lang, Oxford. pp. 227–248.

Kadaplackal, F. (2008), "How the Idea of 'Created Co-Creator Can Contribute to the Norturing of Frugality in Economic Life?" in L. Bouckaert, H. Opdebeeck and L. Zsolnai (Eds): *Frugality: Rebalancing Material and Spiritual Values in Economic Life*. 2008. Peter Lang, Oxford. pp. 71–94.

Max-Neef, M. (1991), *Human Scale Development. Conception, Application and Further Reflections*, Apex Press.

Max-Neef, M. (1992), *Experiences in Barefoot Economics*. Zed Books, London.

Max-Neef, M. (1999), "A Draft Agenda for Economic Recovery and World Development. Reflections on a Paradigm Shift in Economics," in Lyon and Libby (Eds) *The New Economics*. The New Environment Institute, London.

Michaelis, L. (2008), "Quaker Simplicity" in L. Bouckaert, H. Opdebeeck and L. Zsolnai (Eds): *Frugality: Rebalancing Material and Spiritual Values in Economic Life*. 2008. Peter Lang, Oxford. pp. 95–122.

Opdebeeck, H. (2008), "The Urgency of a Frugality-Based Economics" in L. Bouckaert, H. Opdebeeck and L. Zsolnai (Eds): *Frugality: Rebalancing Material and Spiritual Values in Economic Life*. 2008. Peter Lang, Oxford. pp. 185–204.

Sternberg, E. (1999), *The Stakeholder Concept: A Mistaken Doctrine*, NTC Publications, Oxfordshire.

Wicks, A.C., Gilbert, D.R. Jr. and Freeman, R.E. (1994), "A feminist reinterpretation of the stakeholder concept," *Business Ethics Quarterly*, 4 (4), pp. 475–497.

CHAPTER 9

Buddhist Economic Strategy*

> One need not be a Buddhist or an economist to practice Buddhist economics.
>
> — VENERABLE P.A. PAYUTTO, 1994

This paper explores Buddhist economics as a major alternative to the Western economic mindset. Buddhist economics, developed by E.F. Schumacher, Venerable P.A. Payutto, Richard Welford and others, challenges the basic principles of modern Western economics: (i) profit-maximization, (ii) cultivating desires, (iii) introducing markets, (iv) instrumental use of the world, and (v) self-interest-based ethics. Buddhist economics proposes alternative principles such as minimizing suffering, simplifying desires, non-violence, genuine care, and generosity. Buddhist economics is not a system but a strategy, which can be applied in any economic setting. It is argued here that Buddhist economics is rational, ethical, and ecological and can lead to happiness, peace and permanence.

*   First published: "Buddhist Economic Strategy" in L. Bouckaert, H. Opdebeeck and L. Zsolnai (Eds): *Frugality: Rebalancing Material and Spiritual Values in Economic Life*. 2008. Peter Lang, Oxford. pp. 279–303.

1 Why Buddhism?

Thomas Schelling rightly characterizes modern Western economics as an 'egonomical framework'. Modern Western economics is centered on self-interest, understood as satisfaction of the wishes of one's body-mind ego. Buddhism challenges this view because it has a different conception of the self, which is *anatta*, the 'no-self' (Elster 1985).

Anatta specifies the absence of a supposedly permanent and unchanging self. What is normally thought of as the 'self' is nothing more than an agglomeration of constantly changing physical and mental constituents. The *anatta* doctrine attempts to encourage Buddhist practitioners to detach themselves from the misplaced clinging to what is mistakenly regarded as self, and from such detachment (aided by moral living and meditation) the way to *Nirvana* can be successfully traversed.

Modern neuroscience supports the Buddhist view of the self. What neuroscientists have discovered can be called the selfless (or virtual) self, "a coherent global pattern, which seems to be centrally located, but is nowhere to be found, and yet is essential as a level of interaction for the behavior." The nonlocalizable, nonsubstantial self acts as if it were present, like a virtual interface (Varela 1999: 53 & 61).

The Buddhist cosmology has the entire universe at its center in contrast to the anthropocentric worldview of Western culture. For Buddhists human beings are humble in the totality and are essentially just grains of sand in the vast limitless ocean of space.

The *Four Noble Truths* of the Buddha address the dynamics of human life (Welford 2006).

(1) Life is suffering. This has to be comprehended. With the increasing secularism and dissociation from nature and the environment, and rising expectations inside and outside work, people are becoming less satisfied with life and lifestyles.

(2) The cause of suffering is desire. This has to be abandoned. Heightened dissatisfaction arguably has implications for consumerism.

First, there is an erroneous perception that purchasing goods is going to make one happy; and second, we are increasingly dissatisfied and thus unhappy or stressed because we are unable to deal with what is needed to change.

(3) The cessation of suffering is the cessation of desire. This has to be realized. By becoming aware that there is a root to the general societal malaise and avoidance of environmental and social responsibilities, we can understand that there is a way of stopping such complacency and beginning a path to sustainability.

(4) The path to the cessation of desire requires practice. To cease doing what makes us dissatisfied, we have to realize the result of that dissatisfaction and keep trying to behave in a more sustainable manner. Buddhism shows us that this is difficult and requires ongoing commitment and practice.

Even if one gets what one desires, greater desires always emerge. The ego mindset cannot be fulfilled and its greed for more satisfaction and recognition becomes the source of its own destruction. This is a source of suffering because the human spirit becomes captured by the avaricious mind. The way through this life of constantly unsatisfied desires is the practice of nonattachment – in other words, developing a distance from all desires (Welford 2006).

2 Elements of Buddhist Economics

British economist *E.F. Schumacher* was the first to develop the conception of Buddhist economics. In his best-selling book *Small Is Beautiful* Schumacher devotes a whole chapter to describing Buddhist economics as an economics based on the Buddhist way of life (Schumacher 1973). The main goal of a Buddhist life is *liberation* from all suffering. *Nirvana* is the final state, which can be approached by want negation and purification of human character.

Thai Buddhist monk *Venerable P.A. Payutto* summarizes his view on Buddhist economics under the title *A Middle Way for the Market Place* (Payutto 1994).

Payutto believes that Western economics gives rational solutions to largely irrational problems. Buddhist teachings offer profound ideas about the psychology of desire and the motivating forces of economic activity. These insights can lead to a liberating self-awareness that dissolves the confusion between what is truly harmful and what is truly beneficial in production and consumption.

Buddhism differentiates between two kinds of desires. One is *tanha* and the other is *chanda*. Tanha is directed toward feeling; it leads to seeking objects that pander to self-interest and is supported and nourished by ignorance. Chanda is directed toward true well-being; it leads to effort and action and is founded on intelligent reflection. As wisdom develops, chanda becomes more dominant, while the blind craving of tanha loses its strength. By training and developing ourselves, we live less and less at the directives of ignorance and tanha and more under the guidance of wisdom and chanda. This leads to a more skillful life and much better and more fruitful relations with the things around us (Payutto 1994: 13).

From the Buddhist viewpoint, economic activity should be a *means* to a *good* and *noble life*. Production, consumption and other economic activities are not ends; they are means, and the end to which they must lead is the development of well-being within the individual, society and the environment. The major part of our lives is taken up with economic activities. If economics is to have a real part to play in the resolution of human problems, then all economic activities must contribute to well-being and help realize the potential for a good and noble life.

At the heart of Buddhism is the wisdom of *moderation*. In Western economics unlimited desires are controlled by scarcity, but in the Buddhist model they are controlled by an appreciation of moderation and the aim of well-being. The resulting balance will eliminate the harmful effects of uncontrolled economic activity. Whenever we use things – whether they be food, clothing, or even paper and electricity – we can take the time to reflect on their true purpose, rather than using them heedlessly. By reflecting in this way we can avoid overconsumption and understand 'the right amount', the 'middle way'.

Buddhist economics emphasizes that *nonconsumption* can contribute to well-being. Monks eat only one meal a day and strive for a kind of well-being that is dependent on little. Therefore Buddhism recognizes that certain demands can be satisfied through nonconsumption, a position that Western economic thinking would find hard to appreciate. Refraining from eating can play a role in satisfying our nonmaterial, spiritual needs. The path to true contentment involves reducing the artificial desire for sense-pleasure, while encouraging and supporting the desire for quality of life (Payutto 1994: 18 & 19).

In industries where production entails the destruction of natural resources and environmental degradation, nonproduction is sometimes the better choice. To choose, we must distinguish between production with positive results and production with negative results – production that enhances well-being and that which destroys it. In this light, nonproduction can be useful. A person who produces little in materialistic terms may consume much less of the world's resources and lead a life that is beneficial to the world around him or her. Such a person is of more value than one who diligently consumes large amounts of the world's resources while manufacturing goods that are harmful to society. Western economics could never make such a distinction; it would praise a person who produces and consumes (that is, destroys) vast amounts more than one who produces, consumes, and thereby destroys, little (Payutto 1994: 23).

Although Buddhism has been characterized as an ascetic religion, asceticism was rejected by the Buddha. Buddhism judges the ethical value of *wealth* by the way in which it is obtained and the uses to which it is put. Harmful actions associated with wealth can appear in three forms: seeking wealth in dishonest or unethical ways; hoarding wealth for its own sake; and using wealth in ways that are harmful.

Payutto characterizes Buddhist economics as 'Middle Way economics' whose aim is the realization of true well-being by activities that neither harm oneself (by causing a decline in the quality of life) nor others (by causing problems in society or imbalances in the environment).

British economist *Richard Welford* developed a Buddhist economic view with an emphasis on business (Welford 2006).

Welford writes that Buddhism can be the source of greater individual contentment and satisfaction and that this can be consistent with the protection of nature and care of the environment. There is a need to move away from mass consumption economies toward a more environmentally restorative one, and here, lessons from Buddhism can help us to find some solutions.

While modern Western economics stresses self-interest and material development, Buddhist economics would stress interconnectedness and inner development. It would also place an emphasis on culturally appropriate economic approaches. A Buddhist approach involves an emphasis on a much more sustainable development, where human beings and other living creatures could realize their potential, and where inner development and economic development were compatible, all within a just society and healthy ecosystem.

Buddhist economics sees little problem with an economics that is beneficial to oneself, to one's business and to one's country, but only in circumstances of nonharmfulness to others. In other words, establishing mutually beneficial transactions rather than exploitative ones is an important consideration in this approach. Indeed, mutually beneficial activities is a basic tenet that sustains Buddhist economics.

An economics based on respect would help to reverse the mounting ecological crisis. Economics should be based on notions of fair give and take, but this is missing when it comes to the environment, where we seem to have developed a policy of 'take and take' without giving any thought to the consequences of such actions. Put simply, if we are going to take something from the environment we must be prepared to ensure that it can be replaced in one way or another. We need to develop a restorative economy where whatever damage is done to the environment is restored or fully compensated for. We should remember that human beings are not the masters of the universe but only a very small part of it. Therefore it is the earth as a whole rather than human beings that must be placed at the center of our worldview.

Moderation shows the knowledge that Buddhists have, knowing that *things* and consumption are not the root of happiness and contentment.

The search for true happiness is not a material activity. Reaching the goals of happiness and contentment require us all, as individuals, to spend less time consuming and more time contemplating – less time following prescribed roles and more time being creative.

Buddhist economics is neither antibusiness nor antiprofit. It does, however, stress the importance of combining commerce with spiritual practice and sees business as being of considerable potential benefit and impetus for change if conducted along lines of moderation. Moreover, it argues that the work people do is deeply worthwhile and is in itself one path toward happiness and contentment. It calls on individuals engaged in work to reflect their spiritual life in their activities and to be honest in their dealings. It advocates activities that benefit oneself only if they also benefit others, and stresses the need to care for all life and the environment. At all times business activities should be ethical, nonexploitative and nonharmful.

Welford stresses that Buddhist economics is founded on changes at the individual level, which will filter through to institutional change and begin to impact on the activities of governments and businesses. This is promising in some respects because rather than having to wait for radical change through some sort of democratic process, which is unlikely to happen, each of us can begin the process of change now. In developing a spiritual attitude of caring and compassion we can improve our own lives, the lives of others and the planet as a whole (Welford 2006).

3 Principles of Buddhist Economics

3.1 Minimizing Suffering

While modern Western economics promotes doing business based on individual, self-interested, profit-maximizing ways, Buddhism suggests an alternative strategy. The underlying principle of Buddhist economics is to *minimize suffering* of all sentient beings, including nonhuman beings.

From a Buddhist viewpoint a project is worthy to be undertaken if it can reduce the suffering of all those who are affected. Also, any change in economic-activity systems that reduces suffering should be welcomed. The suffering-minimizing principle can be formulated to reveal that the goal of economic activities is not to produce gains but to decrease losses.

The *prospect theory* developed by *Daniel Kahneman* and *Amos Tversky* uncovers the basic empirical features of the value function of decision makers. The central finding of prospect theory is that the value function is concave for gains and convex for losses (Kahneman and Tversky 1979). This regularity is illustrated by the following decision problems.

Problem (I) Choose between
(A)   25% chance to win $6000
(B)   25% chance to win $4000 and 25% to win $2000

Of all subjects, 82 percent chose prospect (B) and only 18 percent of them chose prospect (A). Notice that the expected utility is $1500 in both cases. The next problem is the negative version of problem (I).

Problem (II) Choose between
(C)   25% chance to lose $6000
(D)   25% chance to lose $4000 and 25% to lose $2000

The expected utility is negative $1500 in both cases. But, 70 percent of the subjects chose prospect (C) and only 30 percent of them chose prospect (D).

These disturbing results correspond to the central hypotheses of prospect theory because

$$V(\$6000) < V(\$4000) + V(\$2000)$$

and

$$V(-\$6000) > V(-\$4000) + V(-\$2000),$$

where V( ) is the value function.

A salient characteristic of people's attitudes to changes is that losses loom larger than gains. "The aggravation that one experiences in losing a sum of money appears to be greater than the pleasure associated with gaining the same amount. Indeed, most people find symmetric bets of the form (x, 0.50; -x, 0.50) distinctively unattractive. Moreover, the aversiveness of symmetrically fair bets generally increases with the size of the stake. That is, if x > y > 0, then (y, 0.50; – y, 0.50) is preferred to (x, 0.50; – x, 0.50)" (Kahneman and Tversky 1979: 279).

The main statement of prospect theory is that the value function is steeper for losses than for gains.

That is

$$V(x) \quad < \quad -V(-x)$$

which means that decision makers are more sensitive to losses than to gains.

Experiments show that the ratio of the slopes in the domains of losses and gains, the "loss aversion coefficient," might be estimated as about 2 : 1 (Tversky and Kahneman 1991, 1992).

That is

$$2V(x) \quad \approx \quad -V(-x)$$

Since humans (and other sentient beings) display loss sensitivity, it does make sense trying to reduce losses for oneself and for others rather than trying to increase gains for them. Losses should not be interpreted only in monetary terms or applied only to humans. The capability of experiencing losses, i.e., suffering, is *universal* in the realm of both natural and human kingdoms.

3.2 Simplifying Desires

Modern Western economics cultivates desires. People are encouraged to develop new desires for things to acquire and for activities to do. The profit motive of companies requires creating more demand. But psychological research shows that materialistic value orientation undermines well-being. "People who are highly focused on materialistic values have lower personal well-being and psychological health than those who believe that materialistic pursuits are relatively unimportant. These relationships have been documented in samples of people ranging from the wealthy to the poor, from teenagers to the elderly, and from Australians to South Koreans." These studies document that "strong materialistic values are associated with a pervasive undermining of people's well-being, from low life satisfaction and happiness, to depression and anxiety, to physical problems such as headaches, and to personality disorders, narcissism, and antisocial behavior" (Kasser 2002: 22).

Psychologists call the mechanism through which people seek to satisfy their desires 'auto-projection'. It is a loser strategy, whether or not people achieve their desired goals. When they are not able to reach the goals they envision, they attribute their continuing dissatisfaction to their failure to reach the alleged corrective measures. When they succeed in attaining their goals, this usually does not bring what they hoped for and their feelings of discomfort are not relieved. So striving for satisfying desires never brings people the fulfillment they expect from it (Grof 1998: 207).

The Buddhist strategy is just the opposite of the Western one. It suggests not to multiply but to simplify our desires. Above the minimum material comfort, which includes enough food, clothing, shelter, and medicine, it is wise to try to reduce one's desires. Wanting less could bring substantial benefits for the person, for the community, and for nature.

Hunter-gather societies are instructive examples. In his "Stone Age Economics", *Marsal Sahlins* characterizes Paleolithic communities as the original affluent society. They exercised what Sahlins calls a 'Zen road to affluence'. The Zen strategy is to regard human material wants as finite and few, and technical means unchanging but adequate. In this way people can enjoy an unparalleled material plenty, wanting little and lacking nothing. Their wants are scarce and their means are consequently plentiful (Sahlins 1998).

John Gowdy rightly concludes that modern market capitalism does not reflect human nature. The Western economic mindset is a small minority view among the tens of thousands of cultures that have existed since *Homo sapiens* emerged some 200,000 years ago. Humans lived as hunter-gatherers for almost our entire existence as a species (Gowdy 1998).

Buddhism recommends moderate consumption and is directly aimed at changing one's preferences through meditation, reflection, analyses, autosuggestion and the like. French economist *Serge-Christophe Kolm* developed a formal model to treat consumption and meditation together (Kolm 1985).

In a simplified form his model is as follows: let 'u' represent one's *well-being* (or *sukkha*). Let 'c' and 'tm' represent consumption and meditation, respectively. These variables are linked by the relation $u = u$ (c, tm).

The acquisition of consumption goods takes time, because labor is involved in producing them or money is required to buy them. Let this length of time be 'ta'. The quantity of c is an increasing dependent variable of this, so $c = c(ta)$.

We then have $u = u [c(ta), tm]$. Time should be divided between meditation and working for consumption. What is the optimal allocation of time between these two activities? The Buddha says that the optimum is some meditation, to lower the desire for consumption and to be satisfied with less, and some consumption and the requirement to work that it entails. This is the 'Middle Way'. In economic terms this means "the marginal productivity of labor involved in producing consumption is equal to the marginal efficacy of the meditation involved in economizing upon consumption without altering satisfaction" (Kolm 1985: 240–242).

Desiring less is even fruitful in the case of money. Western economics presupposes that more money is better than less money. But, getting more money may have negative effects. Overpaid employees and managers do not always give high-level performance.

Being underfinanced might be beneficial for a project. If people have smaller budgets, they may use the money more creatively and effectively. *Buddha* had no budget at all for financing his mission.

3.3 Practicing Nonviolence

In his monumental economics textbook, *Paul Samuelson* selected the motto, "Even a parrot can become an economist. All what he should learn is only two words: supply and demand." (Samuelson 1948) Modern Western economics aims to introduce markets wherever social problems need solving.

Karl Polanyi refers to the whole process of marketization as 'The Great Transformation', by which spheres of society became subordinated to the market mechanism (Polanyi 1946). In the age of globalization we can experience this marketization process on a much larger scale and in a speedier way than ever.

The market is a powerful institution. It can provide goods and services in a flexible and productive way; however, it has its own limitations. Limitations of the market come from nonrepresented stakeholders, underrepresented stakeholders, and myopic stakeholders.

Primordial stakeholders such as nature and future generations are simply not represented in the market because they do not have a 'vote' in terms of purchasing power. They cannot represent their interests in the language of supply and demand. Other stakeholders such as the poor and marginalized people are underrepresented because they do not have enough purchasing power to signal their preferences in the market. Finally, stakeholders who are well represented in the market, because they have enough purchasing power, often behave in a myopic way; that is, they heavily discount values in space and time. Market prices usually reflect the values of the strongest stakeholders and favor preferences here and now. Because of these inherent limitations the market cannot give a complete, unbiased direction for guiding economic activities (Zsolnai and Gasparski (eds) 2001).

Nonviolence ('ahimsa') is the main guiding principle of Buddhism for solving social problems. It is required that an act does not cause harm to the doer or the receivers. Nonviolence prevents doing actions that directly cause suffering for oneself or others and urges participative solutions.

The community-economy models are good examples. Communities of producers and consumers are formed to meet both their needs at the lowest cost and reduced risk by a long-term arrangement. Studying dozens of working models, *Richard Douthwaite* characterizes community economy as follows (Douthwaite 1996):

Community economy uses *local resources* to meet the needs of *local people* rather than the wants of markets far away. World prices do not determine what will be produced and the key production processes need to be run entirely without inputs from the world system.

Community economy is based on self-reliance that is closely linked to ecological sustainability. Practically speaking, *living within limits* and sustainability are one and the same thing. Every community should achieve ecological sustainability by exploiting the ecological niche available for itself. Ideally this entails meeting some basic targets as follows.

(A) Every system used in the community should be able to be continued, and every production cycle repeated, without environmental deterioration for hundreds of years.

(B) The size of the community should be stabilized at an appropriate level. The community economy cannot depend on economic growth for the maintenance of jobs and prosperity.

(C) The community must produce at least enough food and raw materials to enable its members to live simple, comfortable lives while staying within the limits of their environment and not exploiting their parts of the world.

(D) All energy used in the community should come from renewable resources.

(E) The community could have its own currency and banking system to avoid being exploited or disrupted from outside. Capital should not allow flowing in or out, and interest rates, if any, should be determined internally.

Characteristics (A),...,(E) define the ideal type of community economy. In the contemporary world it is not easy to approach it; however, there are many practical working models of the community economy, especially in the USA, Australia, Britain, and Ireland.

Community-supported agriculture is the prime example of a community-based economic activity. Its essence is simple: a group of people agrees

to buy, in advance, shares of a farmer's harvest of food grown in an ecologically sound manner. It is a small-scale system whose central decision-making
body is the group composed of the farmer and the consumers. Community-
supported agriculture adopts a long-term perspective – decommodify food
and land, and reject monoculture and chemicals. Community-supported
agriculture strives to foster trust, build value-community and bring people
closer to the land and the farm (Dyck 1994).

Achieving ecological sustainability and nonviolence requires altering
the underlying structure of dominating configurations of modern business.
This means de-emphasizing profit maximization and market systems and
introducing small-scale, locally adaptable, culturally diverse ways of engag-
ing in substantive economic activity.

3.4 Genuine Care

According to the famous saying by *Oscar Wilde*, economists know the price
of everything and the value of nothing. In modern Western economics
the value of an entity (be it human being, other sentient being, object or
anything else) is determined by its marginal contribution to the production output. A project is considered worthy of undertaking if and only if
its discounted cash flow is positive. This instrumental view of the world is
a prime example of the calculating thinking that has been heavily criticized
by *Martin Heidegger*.

For Heidegger calculating thinking ('das rechnende Denken') is at the
bottom of human thinking and conveys disapproval. He writes, "Every-
dayness takes Dasein as a ready-to-hand matter of concern, that is, something managed and reckoned up. 'Life' is a 'business,' whether or not it
covers its costs. (...) Thinking in the sense of calculating (...) roams to and
from only *within* a fixed horizon, within its boundary, although it does
not see it." And Heidegger says that the shopkeeper's thinking is blinkered
because it does not transcend its horizon to reflect on it and on its own
thinking (Inwood 1999: 216).

The basic problem with the instrumental approach is that it generates the worst response from the beings involved. To get the best from the partners requires taking genuine care in their existence.

As we know from Robert Frank's research (Frank 2004) caring organizations are rewarded for the higher costs of their socially responsible behavior by their ability to form commitments among owners, managers and employees and to establish trust relationships with customers and subcontractors.

3.5 Generosity

There is a place for ethics in modern Western economics, but only a little one. The Western economic man is allowed to consider the interest of others only if it serves his or her own interest. The self-interest based, opportunistic approach often fails.

Generosity might work in business and social life because people are 'Homo reciprocans'. They tend to reciprocate what they get and often they give back more in value to the doer than he or she gave to them.

Ernst Fehr and *Simon Gaechter* designed a gift exchange game in which the employer makes a wage offer with a stipulated desired level of effort from the worker. The worker may then choose an effort level, with costs to his or her rising in effort. The employer may fine the worker if his or her effort level is thought to be inadequate. The surplus from the interaction is the employer's profits and the worker's wage minus the cost of effort (and the fine, where applicable).

The self-regarding worker would choose the minimum feasible level of effort, and, anticipating this, the self-regarding employer would offer the minimum wage. But experimental subjects did not conform to this expectation. Employers made generous offers and workers' effort levels were strongly conditioned on these offers. High wages were reciprocated by high levels of efforts (Bowles 2004: 495–496).

4 Not a System but a Strategy

Buddhist economics represents a *minimizing framework* where suffering, desires, violence, instrumental use, and self-interest have to be minimized. This is why "small is beautiful" and "less is more" nicely express the essence of the Buddhist approach to economic questions.

Modern Western economics represents a *maximizing framework*. It wants to maximize profit, desires, market, instrumental use, and self-interest and tends to build a world where "bigger is better" and "more is more" (*Table 1*).

Table 1 *Modern Western Economics versus Buddhist Economics*

Modern Western Economics	Buddhist Economics
maximize profit	minimize suffering
maximize desires	minimize desires
maximize market	minimize violence
maximize instrumental use	minimize instrumental use
maximize self-interest	minimize self-interest
'bigger is better'	'small is beautiful'
'more is more'	'less is more'

Buddhist economics does not aim to build an economic system of its own. Rather, it represents a strategy, which can be applied in any economic setting at any time. It helps to create livelihood solutions that reduce the suffering of all sentient beings through the practices of want negation, nonviolence, caring and generosity.

In his paper "Towards a Progressive Buddhist Economics," *Simon Zadek* asks the important question of whether Buddhist economics is able to penetrate the modern economy to prevent it from driving us along a materially unsustainable path, and to uproot its growing hold on our psychological conditions. And he concludes that we have no choice but to engage in modernization in an attempt to redirect it or at least reduce its negative effects (Zadek 1997).

The *ecological rightsizing of organizations* is a vital issue, which can show how Buddhist economics might work for modern-day business.

Organizations aim to reduce their negative ecological impacts worldwide; however, they do not have a critical measure to judge how much reduction is enough. Using the substantive-economics approach of *Karl Polanyi* and the ecological-footprint analysis developed by *Mathis Wackernagel*, a method can be developed by which the right ecological size of organizations can be determined (Polanyi 1971, Wackernagel and Rees 1996).

The primary function of organizations is to assure or contribute to the livelihoods of those who are involved in the company's activities. For this reason the upper ecological limit for a company should primarily be determined by the globally fair ecological share of its employees.

The *ecological footprint* of an organization is equal with the land and water that is required to support its activities indefinitely using prevailing technology.

Let *Ef(O,t)* be the ecological footprint of organization O in the period of time t. The crucial question is whether this footprint exceeds the fair ecological share of the organization.

The *fair ecological share* of an organization is determined by the 'earthshare' of its employees, taking into account the proportion the output of economic organizations has in the consumption of individuals and the dependency ratio in the economy.

The earthshare is the average amount of ecologically productive land and sea available globally per capita. In 2000 this earthshare was calculated at *1.6 hectare* per person (Chambers, Simmons and Wackernagel 2000: 64–66).

The dependency ratio is the ratio of the economically dependent part of the population to the productive part. The economically dependent part is recognized to be children who are too young to work and individuals who are too old or unable to work.

Let the s(t) be the earthshare of individuals in period t. Let α be the proportion of the output of economic organizations in the total consumption of individuals. Let d be the dependency ratio in the economy. Let us suppose that organization O employs x people.

Then the fair ecological share of organization O is

$$Es(O,t) = \alpha(dx)s(t)$$

If Ef(O,t) > Es(O,t), then organization O is *ecologically overshot*. That is, the organization uses more land and water than it is allowed in a fair distribution of ecological shares.

Es(O,t) – Ef(O,t) is the *ecological deficit* of organization O in period t.

Ef(O,t) / Es(O,t) can be considered a measure of the ecological oversizement of the organization.

Based on this conception, *constructive proposals* can be developed for organizations be they business, public or voluntary entities. Strategies can be identified for ecologically rightsizing organizations; for example, reducing their ecological footprints by introducing new technologies and applying better environmental management systems and/or expanding ecological frontiers through enlarging the workforce.

5 Conclusion

Today's business model is based on and cultivates narrow self-centeredness. Buddhist economics points out that emphasizing individuality and promoting the greatest fulfillment of the desires of the individual conjointly lead to destruction.

Happiness research convincingly shows that not material wealth but the richness of *personal relationships* determines happiness. Not things but people make people happy (Lane 1998). Western economics tries to provide people with happiness by supplying enormous quantities of things.

But what people need are caring relationships and generous love. Buddhist economics makes these values accessible by direct provision.

Peace can be achieved in nonviolent ways. Wanting less can substantially contribute to this endeavor and make it happen easier.

Permanence, or ecological sustainability, requires a drastic cutback in the present level of consumption and production globally. This reduction should not be an inconvenient exercise of self-sacrifice. In the noble ethos of reducing suffering it can be a positive development path for humanity.

References

Bowles, S. (2004), *Microeconomics. Behavior, Institutions, and Evolution*. Russell Sage Foundation, New York and Princeton University Press, Princeton and Oxford.

Chambers, N., Simmons, C. and Wackernagel, M. (2000), *Sharing Nature's Interest. Ecological Footprints as an Indicator of Sustainability*. Earthscan, London and Sterling, VA.

Douthwaite, R. (1996), *Short Circuit. Strengthening Local Economics for Security in an Unstable World*. 1996. The Lilliput Press.

Dyck, B. (1994), "Build in Sustainable Development and They Will Come: A Vegetable Field of Dreams" *Journal of Organizational Change Management* 1994. No. 4. pp. 47–63.

Elster, J. (1985), "Introduction" in J. Elster (Ed): *The Multiple Self*. Cambridge University Press. Cambridge. pp. 1–34.

Frank, R. (2004), "Can Socially Responsible Firms Survive in Competitive Environments?" in R. Frank: *What Price the Moral High Ground? Ethical Dilemmas in Competitive Environments*. Princeton University Press. Princeton and Oxford.

Gowdy, J. (1998), "Back to the Future and Forward to the Past" in John Gowdy (Ed): *Limited Wants, Unlimited Means*. Island Press, Washington, D.C. and Covelo, California.

Grof, S. (1998), *The Cosmic Game. Explorations of the Frontiers of Human Consciousness*. State University of New York Press, Albany.

Inwood, M. (1999), *A Heidegger Dictionary*. Blackwell, Oxford.

Kahneman, D. and Tversky, A. (1979), "Prospect Theory: An Analysis of Decision Under Risk" *Econometrica* 1979 March pp. 263–291.

Kasser, T. (2002), *The High Price of Materialism*. MIT Press. Cambridge, Massachusetts and London, England.

Kolm, S-C. (1985), "The Buddhist Theory of 'No-self'" in J. Elster (Ed): *The Multiple Self*. Cambridge University Press. Cambridge. pp. 233–265.

Lane, R.E. (1998), "The Joyless Market Economy" in A. Ben-Ner and L. Putterman (Eds): *Economics, Values, and Organizations*. Cambridge University Press, Cambridge. pp. 461–488.

Payutto, P.A. (1994), *Buddhist Economics. A Middle Way for the Market Place*. Buddhadhamma Foundation, Bangkok.

Polanyi, K. (1946), *The Great Transformation. Origins of our Time*. Victor Gollancz Ltd., London.

Polanyi, K. (1971), *The Livelihood of Man*. Academic Press, New York.

Sahlins, M. (1998), "The Original Affluent Society" in J. Gowdy (Ed): *Limited Wants, Unlimited Means*. Island Press, Washington, D.C. and Covelo, California.

Samuelson, P. (1948), *Economics: An Introductory Analysis*. McGraw-Hill Book Company, New Jersey.

Schumacher, E.F. (1973), *Small Is Beautiful. Economics as if People Mattered*. Abacus, London.

Tversky, A. and Kahneman, D. (1991), "Loss Aversion in Riskless Choice: A Reference-Dependent Model" *Quarterly Journal of Economics* 1991. pp. 1039–1061.

Tversky, A. and Kahneman, D. (1992), "Advances in Prospect Theory: Cumulative Representation of Uncertainty" *Journal of Risk and Uncertainty* 1992. pp. 297–323.

Varela, F.J. (1999), *Ethical Know-How. Action, Wisdom, and Cognition*. Stanford University Press, Stanford.

Wackernagel, M. and Rees, W. (1996), *Our Ecological Footprint. Reducing Human Impact on the Earth*. New Society Publishers, Gabriola Island, BC and Stony Creek, CT.

Welford, R. (2006), "Tackling Greed and Achieving Sustainable Development" in L. Zsolnai and K.J. Ims (Eds): *Business within Limits: Deep Ecology and Buddhist Economics*. Peter Lang. Oxford. pp. 25–52.

Zadek, S. (1997), "Towards a Progressive Buddhist Economics" in J. Watts, A. Senauke, and S. Bhikku (Eds): *Entering the Realm of Reality: Towards Dharmmic Societies*. INEB, Bangkok. pp. 241–273.

Zsolnai, L. and Gasparski, W. (Eds) (2002), *Ethics and the Future of Capitalism*. Transaction Publishers, New Brunswick & London.

PART 4

Responsible Economizing

CHAPTER 10

Shallow Success and Deep Failure*

In our modern society, we tend to favor and celebrate short-term success, pseudo-solutions and window-dressing activities at the peril of ignoring long-term consequences. An obsessive hunt for short-term gains, often concretized as profit, produces detrimental effects for all life conditions in the long run. In the functioning of today's corporations, and in whole societies as well, we find many activities that result in grave failures rather than the creation of real solutions to pressing problems.

1 The Problem

'A Pyrrhus victory' is a nice metaphor for a seeming success that, all things considered, finally costs too much. The term can be traced back to King Pyrrhus, who won a battle against the Romans in 279 B.C., but the victory was too expensive. It would have been better for the King and his army to avoid that battle. During our modern history we find many similar examples, and one recurring question is how to avoid painful and destructive failures. Can we under certain conditions be better able to know in advance what to do and what to avoid and restrain, and thereby not waste resources or harm man and nature? There are many examples of the strong forces in organizations that work in the direction of treating symptoms rather than

*   First published: "Shallow Success and Deep Failure" in L. Zsolnai and K.J. Ims (Eds) (2006), *Business within Limits: Deep Ecology and Buddhist Economics*. Peter Lang, Oxford. pp. 3–24 (co-author: *Knut J. Ims*).

underlying problems (Cyert and March 1963). One interesting concept formulated by Norwegian philosopher Zappfe (1996) is the distinction between real-solutions and surrogate-solutions. It is typical today to run away from problems (and responsibility) and stick to surrogate or pseudo solutions.

The terms 'shallow' and 'deep' as used here demonstrate the inspiration we received from Arne Naess and his work on Ecosophy. By shallow, Naess means a reformist approach to the relationship between man and nature. The shallow approach represents a conventional anthropocentric perspective in which the central idea is to secure the health and affluence of people. In contrast, the deep approach favors a relational, total field image, looking at organisms as knots in intrinsic relation.

In his opus magnum "On the Tragic", Zappfe (1966) discusses the concerns of the individual entities and a scale of abilities. Concerned individuals (sentient beings) attempt to realize their potential by using their abilities. The abilities may be inadequate (deficiency) or adequate (sufficiency). An interesting issue arises when there is a surplus of ability related to the demands of the situation. Such a surplus of abilities may have destructive consequences. Zappfe cites an example of this in the case of a huge red deer (*megaceros euryceros*) with antlers that grew excessively from generation to generation through natural selection. The huge antlers were at first an important means for the deer's survival because they could be used for protection against other animals. But eventually, the antlers hooked into bushes and trees and became a heavy burden to carry. The antlers gradually became disproportionate to the deer's body. The *strength* became *transformed* into a serious *weakness*. The long-term effect was that this species finally became extinct because of one-sided growth along only one dimension.

This case captures the essence of the tragedy of imbalance of abilities. Deer do not have a choice, but people do.

2 The Fallacy of Misplaced Techno-Centrism

The choice of interpretation determines how we respond to a certain event, and a deeper awareness of and competence in interpreting events, formulating problems and implementing solutions are essential. A theoretical framework by Mitroff (1998) illustrates a systematic way of looking at different kinds of problems and the consequences it has on which solutions we prefer. Mitroff's framework will be used as a point of departure in order to arrive at different solutions to important problems. The logic behind the framework is that although generating knowledge to reach a deeper understanding is a detour, an indirect way to action, deeper insight is essential in finding appropriate solutions for urgent problems.

One fascinating concept used by Mitroff (1998) is the so-called E3 (Type III error) that relates to the problem-formulation process. E3 means *solving the wrong problem precisely*. We need critical thinking to solve the right problem. Even an approximate solution to the right problem is better than an elegant solution to the wrong one. Mitroff asks us to scrutinize the assumptions we hold about the stakeholders, and the importance of picking the right stakeholders, which generally means expanding the set of stakeholders. To manage the important problems in a fruitful way, system thinking is indispensable to avoiding E3.

Mitroff distinguishes among four perspectives one may take on any problem. These perspectives are scientific/technical, interpersonal/social, existential/spiritual and ecological/systemic (Mitroff 1998: 59).

The scientific, technical way of thinking is the dominant perspective in our Western culture, which favors technical or economic solutions. This may easily lead to the so-called 'pig principle': one-dimensional growth that in the long run will change and pervert the quality of the dimension. The more, the bigger, and the faster – the better it is. This assumption frequently leads to serious fallacy, because usually we do not need more of the same, but more of the right things.

We need a blend of efficiency and effectiveness. One example of connecting a technical solution to an existential problem is to see uncertainty in the organization as a bureaucratic problem efficiently solved with more rules. This is a quick and easy solution, which may cause serious dysfunctional effects in the situation because it may stifle ethical reflection and contribute to a reification of rules. Such rules might also create distance among individuals when proximity would have been the better choice. Only under conditions of proximity, and when encountering the other's face, might the moral competencies of empathy and compassion develop as moral impulses capable of discerning what is good or evil (Bauman 1993).

The Mitroff framework is illustrated through examples inspired by Beck's interesting work on "Risk Society" (Beck 1986). We may view the careless use of pesticides in the West, and in particular in the Third World, as a technical solution to a non-technical problem. We call this the *fallacy of misplaced techno-centrism*. The crops and associated profits were expected to increase by use of new toxic chemicals that killed the plants' enemies. So the solution was to use DDT and other chemicals to increase the harvest. In the short run this was an obvious and tangible success, because the artificial fertilizers and chemicals increased the yields per hectare.

In the long run, powerful and latent side effects became visible. The fertility of the soil declined, many plant and animal species disappeared, and the lead content in the milk of nursing mothers increased. These secondary effects undermined the natural basis of agricultural production and created an ecological crisis. The secondary effects struck back like a boomerang. The pesticides used in the Third World returned to the industrialized countries in the imported fruit, tea leaves and cocoa beans. The lesson to be learned was that the problem of unsatisfactory crop yields cannot be solved by artificial, technical means.

The problem might be better defined as a systemic one, with important second- and third-order effects. Some of the pesticides may produce irreversible threats to the life of plants, animals and human beings. It is better to think of the use of pesticides in a systemic way. They intervene in an ecological system in which everything is interdependent. This perspective encourages us to be much more reflective and cautious with the use of new and artificial materials that in the long run may endanger all life and civilization. As Naess suggests, "If we hurt nature, we hurt ourselves" – because nature and man are one – a unity. In this sense the use of pesticides, while having a systemic character, also has an existential effect on peoples' lives. It might even threaten the existence of life on earth.

Although pollution is one of the primary outcomes of advanced chemical plants, these hazardous industries have even more serious effects on the social conditions of people. Beck (1986) maintains that pollution has a democratic effect, because it affects everybody, even the polluter, in the form of a boomerang effect. But the hazardous effects do not affect the perpetrator and the victims equally. It is a known fact that the poor have a 'systematic attraction' to extreme risk. Unemployed people, the poorest of the poor, settle close to the smokestacks of the chemical factories in the industrialized centers of the Third World. Poor people have a higher acceptance rate of extreme risk. Who were living close to Bhopal in India when the Union Carbide plant had a catastrophic outburst of toxic gas? The poor were. In a social perspective, poor people are leaving their local communities and their children to make money where they can. They move to the cities that gradually develop around chemical plants, which initially were localized far from established cities because of their risk potential. "People are living too close to the plant ... We built [it] in 1968 and no people were here. Now the people come closer and closer and we are bothered about this. The waste air made some people sick ..." (Weir 1987). The social and existential conditions for the poor migrants living too close to the chemical plants of transnational corporations are often miserable.

If the problem of unsatisfied employees is defined as a technical problem, paying higher salaries might solve it. The underlying assumption here is that the most important incentives for man are external, and money is the primary motivational factor. This assumption corresponds well with the view of man as an empty shell equipped with rational preferences. There are, however, several examples demonstrating that the use of monetary incentives can press out intrinsic motivation and lead to reduced activity (Frey 1997).

The Danish philosopher Knud Løgstrup has been heavily inspired by Kierkegaard but strongly argues against some of his writings. Løgstrup cites the phenomenological conditions of man as consisting of compassion, trust, love (in the meaning of eros), the propensity for speech to openness and, finally, fidelity (Løgstrup 1971). According to Løgstrup, we, as human beings, are in a profound sense interdependent. This implies that in any relationship we are vulnerable, due to the exertions of the other's power. Løgstrup writes that we put ourselves into the hands and power of other persons, and in any life encounter the self is confirmed, increased or reduced. Any encounter has effects on our self-image and our self-respect. Thus, our selves are always vulnerable to others. According to Løgstrup, trust is the way of living with anxiety.

Sartre focuses on the other's gaze, and he illustrates in a dramatic manner that a person is not an object but a relation. One of his main postulates is that any human is free, because in every moment we can step back (*se recule*) and reflect upon ourselves, and as a result we are able to transcend ourselves. Freedom implies responsibility, even if most people, according to Sartre, try to avoid freedom as well as responsibility. Emmanuel Levinas (1985) assumes a non-symmetrical responsibility for the *Other* (see also Kemp 1992). This asymmetric relationship belongs to the basic constitutions of the responsible subject. Levinas postulates that a person has a responsible relationship toward all human beings; the self of a person is born out of a union with other persons, stretching itself towards the other – living *for* the other, not only with the other.

Arne Naess (1989) develops the concept of self further. He assumes an ontology that implies that human beings are one with all nature, and that self-realization cannot be attained without taking a much deeper and broader perspective. Through identification with others, you arrive at self-realizing consciousness, and your own self-realization depends on whether other beings have attained self-realization. As a consequence, non-violence as a general principle becomes essential. Naess' deep ecology is highly inspired by Buddhism, wherein the self does not have absolute boundaries. Everything has a living, flowing connection with everything else and there are no isolated entities. To ignore our dependency on our close partnerships with other forms of life has contributed to the creation of a master-slave role, which leads to the alienation of man from himself (Rothenberg 1989).

According to Zappfe (1996), abilities involve under certain conditions an inclination to manifestation, converting the capabilities into action. The abilities may be inadequate (deficiency) or adequate (sufficiency). An interesting case arises when there is a surplus of ability in relation to the demands of the situation, as indicated by the example of the giant antlers of the aforementioned, now-extinct deer. Human capabilities might also be detrimental to life in their maximal manifestation. Surplus in technical efficiency (material culture) is one example. The problem may arise when all material needs are satisfied, but the production of means does not stop. The capabilities get out of control and the tools – the means – become predominant. It is no longer the need that cries for the appropriate means, but the means that cry for a need. The supply exceeds the demand. The means become the goals and shadow for the purpose for which they should be used. We may with Zappfe say that technical insight and competence is exploited for a destructive purpose.

It is an existential fact that we have to live and choose within a world in which we do not know the consequences of our actions. Because our mega-technological means have become so powerful, we have to stop and reflect upon the situation of the Earth (Jonas 1984). Technology is double-faced and can lead to either good or evil. And even its good consequences have the potential of becoming perverted due to excessive growth along one or a few dimensions. "Thus moral responsibility demands that we take into consideration the welfare of those who, without being consulted, will later be affected by what we are doing now. Without our choosing it, responsibility becomes our lot due to the sheer extent of the power we exercise daily ..." (Jonas 1996: 99). Even with the best intentions, we may face long-term effects that are detrimental for future generations and all life on Earth. We need to be aware of this new magnitude of responsibility that we bear.

We need scientific and technological knowledge, but we also need a better understanding of the existential conditions of human beings to avoid the fallacy of defining most problems as economic/scientific and solving them in purely technical ways. We should gain a better understanding of self-realization and what self-realization means in the perspective of deep ecology and sustainability.

3 Toward Real Solutions

Here we summarize the main messages what deep ecology and Buddhist economics can offer for solving the most pressing problems of business, economic and social life in our contemporary world.

3.1 Self-realization

Arne Naess (1989) points out that *self-realization* is the realization of the deeper and broader self. It is identification with or seeing something of yourself in others. Your feelings are somehow adapted to those you identify with. This identification can extend to your friends, your neighbors and your country. It can even extend to the whole of humanity. You can also identify yourself with animals, plants and other natural elements. Through identification with others you find self-realization.

Self-digging means not developing the depth and broadness of the self and instead 'digging' down to ego-fulfillment, as opposed to actualizing oneself through self-realization. You develop a cult of your own self-seeking. You have a reputation, a social image that enhances the feeling that you are somebody who does not need anybody else. Ultimately, you cut off identification with others to such an extent that you are left alone.

Diversity in every aspect of our existence should be a norm, whether it be biodiversity, cultural diversity or economic diversity. Diversity of ideas is also important. If we were to think that there is only one correct idea, one absolute truth, one right way to sustainability, then we might end up creating a form of eco-fascism. It is only through multiplicity, plurality, diversity and inclusivity that we can find self-realization. There is no one final definition of self-realization. We all find our own meaning in this word. It is through practice that we find realization. Just as we all have our own bodies, we all have our own 'realization' (Naess 1989).

Nel Hoftsra and Aloy Soppe (2006) note that deep ecologists go further than the more pragmatic environmental reformers and revisionists, who stress conservation and efficient use of resources and promote a more effective use of nature. They criticize the theoretical assumptions of modern economics and meet the weaknesses and contradictions in the 'dominant social paradigm' of capitalism. Deep ecology can only exist if people act according to nature rather than making nature subordinate to human beings.

A *life according to nature* implies several directives: (i) to discern and respect 'reason' in all things and life (system-thinking), (ii) to discern and respect 'law' in all things and life (cyclical thinking), and (iii) to discern and respect the 'divine' in all things and life (soul and humility) (Hoftsra and Soppe 2006).

Richard Welford (2006) stresses that there are many intrinsically valuable aspects of our lives that could be developed: love and appreciation of nature for its own sake, appreciation of aesthetics, honesty and integrity, self-respect and respect for others, humility, generosity, understanding and knowledge. An emphasis on economic growth and materialism has often led to little space for the development of these aspects of human existence.

We must recognize that self-esteem should come from who we are inside. Not external factors, but factors within our selves provide meaning, security, value and self-worth. None of this can be based on the human ego, only developed through a process of humility and inner development (Welford 2006).

3.2 Greed

Welford (2006) also states that the *ecological crisis* in which we find ourselves is a manifestation of a mindset that fails to recognize interconnectedness and complexity. Human beings, through their materialism, consumption and greed, are directly responsible for most of the unsustainable practices that we see. If there is to be a real move toward sustainable development, it will not be enough to rely on businesses, governments and other institutions. Change will have to occur within people and especially within those of us who live in the West.

In Western economies, people seem to believe that the pursuit of *money* and *material possessions* is the path toward greater happiness, satisfaction and contentment. But in many cases, no matter how wealthy people become or how high their standard of living, they often die without realizing contentment. Indeed, the greedier we become, the less likely we are to find happiness and contentment (Welford 2006).

Nel Hofstra and Aloy Soppe (2006) note that in our contemporary world, the primary function of money and capital (i.e., its role as unit of account and unit of exchange) threatens to become subordinate to the *creation* of *financial wealth* as a *goal in itself*. A high interest rate increases pressure for economic growth in order to make the direct investment profitable. This accelerates pressure on future environmental resources and employee performance. A greedy and sometimes 'violent' approach to future growth generates uncontrolled expectations and volatility of market prices.

3.3 Economism

Ove Jakobsen and Stig Ingebrigtsen (2006) point out that throughout the last few decades, an increasing number of societal sectors have been subjected to privatization and the market economy in the quest to reach goals connected to economic efficiency. This trend is characterized as 'economism'. *Economism* means that the economic value system plays a dominating role in society, ignoring or reducing other values.

The economic invasion of the life-world not only leads to an impairment of culture but also undermines creativity and thrust, two important pillars of the market economy. When economics invades culture, instrumental rationality replaces communicative rationality, functionality represses intentionality, atomistic competition destroys integrated cooperation, consumption becomes more important than cultivation, and utility-converted-to-a-monetary-scale replaces value pluralism (Jakobsen and Ingebrigtsen 2006).

Zsolt Boda (2006) refers to *Karl Polanyi*, who, in his seminal work *The Great Transformation*, argues that the market economy requires a market society, where social interactions and activities such as labor and human relations, the cultivation of land, the management of natural resources, and even the evolution of culture, are coordinated by the logic of the market. Polanyi argues that the social and environmental consequences of this process are dramatic, because a single logic rules over all others (Polanyi 1946).

3.4 Economic Theory

John Gowdy (2006) points out that at the core of traditional economic theory is a concept of human nature that is devoid of social context, mechanically rational, and driven by an insatiable appetite for material possessions. The only outlet for human creativity and self-realization is the consumption of market goods. Responding to the desires of such a creature (*Homo economicus*) in order to maximize profits is the only ethical responsibility of business.

Research in behavioral economics and game theory has already shown that the self-centered model of *Homo economicus* is a poor characterization of human behavior. The evolutionary feasibility of strong reciprocity, that is, cooperative behavior not based on reciprocal altruism, is demonstrated. Also, experimental results and case studies show that sharing is a part of "normal" human behavior (Gowdy 2006).

3.5 Relational ontology

Julie Nelson (2006) notes that deep ecology and Buddhism share a thoroughly *relational ontology*. In both deep ecology and Buddhist philosophy, what really *is* are relations and processes. Things exist in a state of dependence on the relations that constitute them. The diversity and elaboration of these relations and processes has value. The intrinsic worth of relationality, and the responsiveness of humans to this worth through gratitude, compassion, and care, form the basis for ethics which permeates the ground of being.

Modern *Western thought* is based on a *substantivist ontology*. Relations are seen as secondary – as simply the way that pre-existing 'stuff' is arranged in patterns with, or bounces against, other 'stuff'. Since the rise of modern science, the physical world has been conceived of as a sort of ethically neutral clockwork, driven by the 'laws' of physics. Some modern thinkers try to take a thoroughly reductionistic approach, seeing all issues of ethics, aesthetics and emotions as simply the epiphenomena of indifferent processes of evolution.

The insights of relationality extend to big, human-made and materially oriented institutions such as corporations and economies. Recognition of symmetric mutuality opens our thinking to ways in which co-workers might treat one another with respect. The recognition of asymmetric mutuality further opens up the possibility of thinking about relations of respect among people with different levels of power and different roles. Not all workers in an enterprise have equal abilities in leadership, inventiveness, or finance. Enterprises can be structured in ways that take advantage of people's different qualities of power, while still retaining a fundamental attitude of mutuality (Nelson 2006).

3.6 Material Flow Analyses

Peter Daniels (2006) emphasizes that "material flow analysis" covers several distinctive approaches. But they are directed toward the systematic physical measurement of the magnitude and 'location' of material (and energy) flows. The flows cover environmentally significant materials as they move through the socioeconomic metabolism of human geographic systems. The main assumption is that the *impact* of *human economic activity* is a *physical phenomenon* caused by the magnitude, concentration, dissipation, and transformation of flows of material and energy.

Material flow analysis as the systematic analysis of the physical environmental consequences of livelihood activities is a way to identify how and where the socio-economy can be transformed into a more sustainable form. It serves as an important methodology for making *eco-restructuring strategies* the best prospect for operationalizing sustainable development.

The most important link between Buddhist economics and material flow analysis is that both are predicated on reducing the metabolism of human economies. The Buddhist view calls for minimum environmental intervention and human-induced material flows and transformations. An economic system founded on this caution would be supportive of technological and consumption-related savings of material and energy, recycling of products and waste (including closed-loop, integrated production systems), and the reduced toxicity and physical flows of pollution.

Physical growth in intervention will create imbalance and ecosystem instability. Flow accounting based on metabolism reduction, and Buddhist economics, are both built on comparable natural law principles that 'scientifically' prescribe minimum disruption and violence, and livelihood and consumption patterns that are in harmony and balance with the external world (Daniels 2006).

3.7 Dialogue between Culture and Economics

Ove Jakobsen and Stig Ingebrigtsen (2006) stress the importance of *dialogues* based on the principles of *discursive rationality* as a tool to combine the cultural life-world with the economic system without undermining either of them.

Dialogues involving all relevant stakeholders represent a force for changing the direction of development and domesticating the undesirable effects of market forces. Meanings are created, knowledge is developed, and learning takes place in the dialogue among different stakeholders. Dialogue-based relationships among the actors might contribute to strengthening values like sympathy and empathy, and to using learning and innovation as productive forces.

In the process of coordinating the interplay among the different stakeholders, a new institutional setting is proposed – *the communicative arena*. In the communicative arena, the agents concord their "strong evaluations" through processes based on communicative rationality and coordinate their economic actions to bring about common ends. Sustainable development presupposes an arena where economic and cultural agents coordinate and evaluate their different values and norms through communicative processes (Jakobsen and Ingebrigtsen 2006).

3.8 Environmental commons

Zsolt Boda (2006) argues that we need *complex institutional arrangements* for securing the *global environmental commons*. Privatizing them is not a good solution. It pretends to provide incentives for protecting the commons but just the opposite happens: it voids the concept of the commons of its inherent ethical content.

Business must acknowledge and respect the inherent value of the commons. This claim implies the following three correlative *duties*: (i) Business shall refrain from appropriating common resources. (ii) Business shall take part in the governance of the commons and contribute to effective regimes to govern and manage them. (iii) Business shall contribute financially to the maintenance of the commons (Boda 2006).

3.9 Theory of the Firm

Julie Nelson (2006) argues that limiting possible relationships to either arms-length contracts or hierarchical control rules out the idea that values, group identity, mutuality, non-hierarchical structures or ethics could play a role within and among contemporary business organizations. Yet the evidence on employee behavior suggests otherwise. Real humans do not simply leave their needs for social relations, their values, their loyalties and their creativity at the workplace door. Many managers and researchers in organizational behavior share the insight that people work better when they are supported, empowered, and allowed to draw on their own creativity than when they are consistently treated as potential shirkers who have to be brought under control.

Buddhist thinking does not prescribe replacement of for-profit businesses with systems of small-scale and cooperative enterprises as the cure for economic suffering. The ethical merit of organizations cannot be prejudged on the basis of size alone, or by the purposes written on their articles of incorporation. Organizations must be evaluated by what they do. Small, purportedly "loving" families are too often the sites of domestic violence. Small non-profit hospitals too often exploit their own workers for the sake of keeping costs in line. Large, for-profit corporations have at times taken actions that show that they can be good workplaces and responsible members of social and environmental communities – when given a chance and especially when encouraged in these directions by consumer, shareholder, and political activism (Nelson 2006).

3.10 Personal Responsibility

Knut Ims (2006) points out that *business* as a human and existential enterprise is a *personal* and *social activity*, and it consists of webs of interpersonal relationships and widespread cooperation. Emotions are a central feature of a person's character. It is the emotions and personal values that constitute persons as extended selves and enable them to identify with a larger community. *Personal responsibility* is not reducible to social, professional or organizational roles. Its essence is to respond to different stakeholders through an authentic and active dialogue (Ims 2006).

3.11 Ecology of Spirit

Mike Bell (2006) stresses that we should see organizations in the context of the living universe. The 'Ecology of Spirit' refers to a complex set of relationships and systems, infused with an inner life-force (or Spirit), that links the land and its creatures to individuals, people, communities, organizations, and to the entire universe.

If the land is living, and we are living, then our organizations must also be living. They have unique Spirits that are linked to our culture. Our organizations can only be as healthy as our culture; and our culture can only be as healthy as our organizations. As members of organizations, we are called to represent and serve our people and to care for and nurture the Spirit of our organizations. We must find a way of realigning our primary relationships and maintaining a balance of Spirit. Our primary relationships are our relationships with these: (i) the Spirit of the land, (ii) our own inner Spirit, (iii) the Spirit of our human community: our families, relatives and the people who are closest to us, and (iv) the Spirit within our organizations and workplaces (Bell 2006).

References

Bauman, Z. (1993), *Postmodern Ethics* Blackwell, Oxford.

Beck, U. (1986), *Risk Society. Towards a New modernity*. Sage publications, London.

Bell, M. (2006), "Toward an Ecology of Spirit" in L. Zsolnai and K.J. Ims (Eds): *Business within Limits: Deep Ecology and Buddhist Economics*. Peter Lang, Oxford. pp. 269–296.

Boda, Zs. (2006), "Respecting the Commons" in L. Zsolnai and K.J. Ims (Eds): *Business within Limits: Deep Ecology and Buddhist Economics*. Peter Lang, Oxford. pp. 167–192.

Cycrt, R. and March, J. (1963) *A Behavioral Theory of the Firm*, Englewood Cliffs, New York.

Daniels, P. (2006), "Reducing Society's Metabolism" in L. Zsolnai and K.J. Ims (Eds): *Business within Limits: Deep Ecology and Buddhist Economics*. Peter Lang, Oxford. pp. 103–147.

Frey, B.S. (1997), *Not Just for the Money. An Economic Theory of PersonalMotivation*. Edward Elgar Publishing, Cheltenham.

Gowdy, J. (2006), "Business Ethics and the Death of 'Homo Oeconomicus'" in L. Zsolnai and K.J. Ims (Eds): *Business within Limits: Deep Ecology and Buddhist Economics*. Peter Lang, Oxford. pp. 83–101.

Hoftsra, N. and Soppe, A. (2006), "Finance as if NAture Mattered" in L. Zsolnai and K.J. Ims (Eds): *Business within Limits: Deep Ecology and Buddhist Economics*. Peter Lang, Oxford. pp. 149–165.

Ims, K.J. (2006), "Take it Personally" in L. Zsolnai and K.J. Ims (Eds): *Business within Limits: Deep Ecology and Buddhist Economics*. Peter Lang, Oxford. pp. 219–268.

Jakobsen, O. and Ingebrigtsen, S. (2006), "Economics and Culture" in L. Zsolnai and K.J. Ims (Eds): *Business within Limits: Deep Ecology and Buddhist Economics*. Peter Lang, Oxford. pp. 57–82.

Jonas, H. (1984), *The Imperative of Responsibility. In Search of an Ethics for the Technological Age*. The University of Chicago Press, Chicago.

Kemp, P. (1992), *Levinas*, Forlaget ANIS, Denmark.

Levinas, E. (1985), *Ethics and Infinity* (Conversations with Philippe Nemo. Translated by R.A. Cohen), Duquesne University Press, Pittsburgh.

Løgstrup, K.E. (1971), *The Ethical Demand*, Fortress Press, Philadelphia (Originally 1956).

Mitroff, I. (1998), *Smart Thinking for Crazy Times. The Art of Solving the Right Problems*, Berrett-Koehler Publishers, Inc. San Francisco.

Naess, A. (1989), *Ecology, Community and Lifestyle. Outline of an Ecosophy*. Cambridge University Press, Cambridge.

Nelson, J. (2006), "The Relational Firm: A Buddhist and Feminist Analysis" in L. Zsolnai and K.J. Ims (Eds): *Business within Limits: Deep Ecology and Buddhist Economics*. Peter Lang, Oxford. pp. 195–217.

Perrow, C. (1984) *Normal Accidents. Living With High-Risk Technologies*. Basic Books, Inc N.Y.

Polanyi, K. (1946), *The Great Transformation. Origins of our Time*. Victor Gollancz Ltd., London.

Reinert, E.S. (Ed.) (2001), *Evolutionary Economics and Income Inequality*, Edward Elgar, Cheltenham.

Weir, D. (1987), *The Bhopal Syndrome. Pecticides, Environment and Health*, Center for Investigative Reporting. Sierra Club Books, San Francisco.

Welford, R. (2006), "Tackling Greed and Achievening Sustainable Development" In L. Zsolnai and K.J. Ims (Eds): *Business within Limits: Deep Ecology and Buddhist Economics*. Peter Lang, Oxford. pp. 25–53.

Zapffe, P.W. (1996), *On the Tragic*. Pax Forlag AS, Oslo (in Norwegian).

Respect for Future Generations*

Future generations are human beings who are yet to be born. Practically, we can imagine them as people who may live in the next 200 years. Activities of present generations may affect the fate of future generations for better or worse. What we do with our natural and cultural heritage mainly determines the way future generations may live their own lives in the future. As currently living human beings, we have an undeniable moral responsibility toward future human beings.

1 Our Obligations to Future Generations

Hans Jonas argued that the ethics of responsibility involves not only the existence of future human beings but also the way they exist. The conditions of the existence of future generations should not cause their capacity of *freedom* and *humanness* to disappear. "Thus moral responsibility demands that we take into consideration the welfare of those who, without being consulted, will later be affected by what we are doing now. Without our choosing it, responsibility becomes our lot due to the sheer extent of the power we exercise daily." (Jonas 1996).

We have natural responsibility toward future generations because our actions and policies affect their possibility of life without being consulted.

---

* First published: "Respect for Future Generations" in L. Bouckaert and P. Arena (Eds) (2010), *Respect and Economic Democracy*. Garant, Antwerp/Apeldoorn pp. 29–36. Republished with the permission of Garant Publishers.

We should consider every generation as equal and should not presuppose anything about the preferences of future generations.

Edith Brown Weiss developed three principles which underline our obligations to future generations (Brown Weiss 1989).

(1) Each generation should be required to conserve the diversity of the natural and cultural resource base, so that it does not unduly restrict the options available to future generations in solving their problems.

(2) Each generation should be required to maintain the quality of the planet so that it is passed on in no worse condition than the present generation received it.

(3) Each generation should provide access to the legacy from past generations to future generations.

2 Accounting for Future Generations

The *Stiglitz, Sen and Fitoussi Report* on the Measurement of Economic Performance and Social Progress presents an advanced view on sustainability, that is, the possibility of permanence of present activities (Stiglitz, Sen and Fitoussi 2009: 61–62).

The report says that sustainability poses the challenge of determining whether we can hope to see the current level of well-being at least maintained for future periods or future generations, or whether the most likely scenario is that it will decline. The idea is the following: the well-being of future generations compared to ours will depend on what resources we pass on to them. Many different forms of resource are involved here. Future well-being will depend upon the magnitude of the stocks of exhaustible resources that we leave to the next generations. It will depend also on how well we maintain the quantity and quality of all the other renewable natural resources that are necessary for life. From a more economic point of view, it will also depend upon how much physical capital – machines and buildings – we pass on, and how much we devote to the constitution of the human capital of future generations, essentially through expenditure on education and research. And it also depends upon the quality of the institutions that we pass on to them, which is still another form of 'capital' that is crucial for maintaining a properly functioning human society.

The question is how can we measure whether enough of these assets will be left or accumulated for future generations? In other words, when can we say that we are currently living above our means?

The Stiglitz, Sen and Fitoussi Report suggests that in order to measure sustainability we need indicators that inform us about the change in the quantities of the different factors that matter for future well-being. Put differently, sustainability requires the simultaneous preservation or increase in several 'stocks': quantities and qualities of natural resources, and of human, social and physical capital (Stiglitz, Sen and Fitoussi 2009: 17).

I agree with the view that what really counts for the well-being of future generations is the quantities and qualities of different stocks or capitals. However, we think we should provide a definition of "sustainability thresholds" for these stocks or capitals in order to evaluate the current state of affairs (Zsolnai et al. 2009).

If the state of a certain stock or capital is below its defined sustainability threshold then it indicates that the present generations pose burdens on future generations in this field. Similarly, if the state of a certain stock or capital is above its defined sustainability threshold then it indicates that the present generations give gifts to future generations in this field. Being identical with the defined sustainability threshold means that the impacts of the present generations are neither negative nor positive for future generations in the given field.

In our model the state of ecological capital, financial capital, human capital, and intellectual capital together determine the fate of future generations. The better the states of these capitals, the better the prospects of future generations, and vice versa.

We developed key indicators for measuring the performance of present generations for future generations (*Table 1*).

Table 1 *Future Generations Indicators*

Capital	Indicator	Value Range	Required Value
Ecological	ecological footprint	0.1–12 ha per capita	< 1,6 ha per capita
Financial	debt service per capital formation	0 – 1,2	< 0,5
Human	share of youths per inactive adults	0,1 – 1,1	> 0,5
Intellectual	investment in research and development	0 – 0,04 of GDP	>0,02 of GDP

Values of the above indicators for selected European countries are shown in *Table 2*.

Table 2 *The Performance of European Countries for Future Generations in 2005*

	Ecological capital (%)	Financial capital (%)	Human capital (%)	Intellectual capital (%)
Austria	-335	?	-187	+86
Belgium	-346	?	-155	-105
Bulgaria	-183	-155	-183	-392
Cyprus	-428	?	-154	-541
Czech Republic	-361	+36	-201	-156
Denmark	-541	?	-174	+76
Estonia	-430	+92	-195	-220
Finland	-353	?	-175	+58
France	-332	?	-152	+93
Germany	-284	?	-202	+80
Great Britain	-359	?	-173	-106

Greece	-394	?	-187	-345
Holland	-295	?	-171	-127
Hungary	-239	-181	-161	-227
Italy	-320	?	-174	-175
Ireland	-287	?	-148	-165
Poland	-267	-118	-168	-345
Latvia	-235	-115	-204	-476
Lithuania	-215	+81	-168	-263
Luxemburg	-810	?	-149	-110
Malta	-322	?	-142	-690
Portugal	-299	?	-198	-256
Romania	-193	+62	-172	-500
Spain	-386	?	-197	-180
Sweden	-343	?	-186	+53
Slovakia	-221	+88	-177	-377
Slovenia	-300	?	-208	-124

From the data several observations can be derived. There is no country in Europe which would not present some burden for future generations in one or more domain. There are some countries (Bulgaria, Hungary, Poland, Latvia) which present burdens in all domains for future generations. There are other countries (Austria, Finland, France, Germany, Sweden, the Czech Republic, Estonia, Romania, Slovakia, Lithuania) which present gifts for future generations in financial or intellectual domains but at the same time present serious ecological and/or human burden for them. The sad fact is that the fate of future generations are not assured in Europe at all.

Caring for future generations is not just an altruistic concern. Improving the position of future generations enhances the future of the present generations too. There is a future for Europe if and only if the prospects of future generations improve throughout Europe.

References

Brown Weiss, E. (1989), *In Fairness to Future Generations: International Law, Common Patrimony, and Intergeneration Equity*. The United Nations University, Tokyo & Transnational Publishers, Inc. Dobbs Ferry, New York.

Jonas, H. (1996), "Toward an Ontological Grounding of an Ethics for the Future" in H. Jonas: *Mortality and Morality. A Search for the Good After Auschwitz*. Northwestern University Press, Evanston, Illinois. pp. 99–112.

Stiglitz, J., Sen, A. and Fitoussi, J-P. (2009), *Report by the Commission on the Measurement of Economic Performance and Social Progress*. http://www.stiglitz-sen-fitoussi.fr (accessed 15/01/2013).

Zsolnai, L. et al. (2009), *The Fate of Future Generations in Hungary*. Business Ethics Center, Corvinus University of Budapest (manuscript).

CHAPTER 12

The Ethics of Systems Thinking*

Systems thinking is represented by the pioneering works of *West E. Churchman, Russell Ackoff, Ian Mitroff,* and others. In this paper I explore ethical assumptions and implications of system thinking with reference to social and environmental decision making.

Influenced by systems thinking *Jozsef Kindler*, professor of decision sciences and co-founder of the Business Ethics Center at Corvinus University of Budapest, developed a new methodology for multidimensional decision making (Kindler and Papp 1977). Kindler's methodology is designed for multi-criteria evaluation of complex systems. It can serve as a prime illustration of the ethical agenda of systems thinking.

I focus on three crucial elements of the Kindler's methodology:

(i)   the completeness of evaluation criteria;
(ii) the measurement of evaluation criteria;
(iii) the problem of disqualification.

*   First published: "The Ethics of Systems Thinking" in Ove Jakobsen and Lars Jacob Tymes Pedersen (Eds) (2011), *Responsibility, Deep Ecology and the Self – Festschrift in Honor of Knut J. Ims*. Oslo, Forlag 1, pp. 17–23. Republished with the permission of Forlag 1 Publisher.

1 The Completeness of Evaluation Criteria

In the case of a complex system we should consider *all* the important aspects of the system and create appropriate evaluation criteria for them. For example, if the system in question is a touristic project which transforms the local ecosystem and the culture of local community, it is not enough to study the direct capital investment, job creation, and the expected tourists flow but one should also consider the longer term ecological, social, and cultural impacts of the project.

In Hungary in 2008–2010 a group of American and Israeli investors wanted to develop a huge gambling and holiday complex called the 'King's City'. The complex consisted of five thousand newly built apartments in a nearly natural environment, at *Lake Velence*, 60 km south-west of Budapest. The project was 2 billion $ and expected to generate a good return on the invested capital in some years. However, it would destroy the nearby ecosystems and drastically transform the life of local people with an increasing traffic of gamblers and the corresponding criminal activities, including drugs and prostitution. The area represents one of the most vulnerable parts of Hungarian society. It is populated by low income people and poor holiday-makers. The territory is important for the whole of Hungary because of the historical and cultural sites nearby. Some considered the King's City project as "raping the soul of Hungary," an effort which attempts to force Hungarian people into serving Western and Middle-Eastern extravagant rich.

2 The Measurement of Evaluation Criteria

Every evaluation criterion should be measured by its own scale. It can be an absolute scale, an interval scale, or an ordinal scale. Influenced by the economic cost-benefit analysis, today's evaluation practice tends to measure everything in terms of money. Decision makers usually disregard those criteria which are not measurable by money. Or they use quasi-market valuation techniques for assessing them. This habit is rather problematic because it transforms lower scale measurement entities into the absolute scale measurement of money.

In multidimensional decision making it is suggested that we should use the so-called 5 points Lickert scale which represents the ordinal scale of measurement. System S for evaluation criterion E can yield the following values:

$$(1)\ E(S) = \begin{array}{ll} 5 & \text{if system S is very good according to E} \\ 4 & \text{if system S is good according to E} \\ 3 & \text{if system S is neutral according to E} \\ 2 & \text{if system S is bad according to E} \\ 1 & \text{if system S is very bad according to E} \end{array}$$

Higher level (absolute or interval scale) measures can be transformed into the ordinal scale and can be compared with lower level measures. In this way decision makers are able to give justice to the more qualitative aspects of the decision situation. The exercise is consistent with the philosophy of social choice advocated by Amartya Sen in his book *The Idea of Justice* (Sen 2009).

In the case of the King's City project economic, ecological, social, and cultural aspects should be distinguished. Economic criteria are measurable by money on the absolute scale of measurement but ecological, social, and cultural criteria can only be measured on the lower scale, that is on the ordinal scale of measurement.

Let K be the King's City project and $-K$ be the non-realization of the project. Let B, E, S, C be the economic, ecological, social, and cultural aspects of the project. Based on the extensive studies of the project we can say that the evaluations of the state of affairs with and without the project are as follows:

$$(2)\ V(K) = [B(K) = 5, E(K) = 1, S(K) = 2, C(K) = 1]$$

(3) $V(-K) = [B(-K) = 1, E(-K) = 5, S(-K) = 4, C(-K) = 5]$

This means that the project is highly beneficial from the business point of view but it is very bad from the ecological and cultural point of view, and bad from the social point of view. The non-realization of the project is very bad from the business point of view but good from the social point of view, and very good from the ecological and cultural point of view.

The decision problem is whether V(K) or V(-K) should be preferred. This is not a trivial problem if we do not permit aggregation across the diverse value dimensions. The no-aggregation rule implies that a gain in one dimension cannot compensate a loss in another dimension.

3 The Problem of Disqualification

There is no super system, that is a system which would be superior to any other system considering all the relevant value dimensions. Every complex system has some disadvantages in comparison to other systems. Kindler and others suggest using the so-called *disqualification coefficient*, a measure which shows in % terms how a given system is worse than the other systems by comparison.

Calculating the disqualification coefficient for the realization and the non-realization of the King's City project we can get:

(4) $\delta(K) = 75\%$

(5) $\delta(-K) = 25\%$

(4) and (5) mean that K is worse than -K in 75% of the evaluation criteria while -K is worse than K in 25% of the the evaluation criteria. It implies that there are considerable disadvantages in realizing the project.

We should set a maximum level for disadvantages, that is define the level of acceptable disadvantages for a system. This logic is different from the philosophy of cost-benefit analysis which says that a system is acceptable if its advantages are greater than its disadvantages. In the multidimensional decision making framework a system is acceptable if and only if its disadvantages do not exceed a certain level.

The decision rule 'elimination by aspect' described by the late Stanford decision psychologist Amos Tversky expresses a similar insight (Tversky 1972). A system is unacceptable for the decision makers if there are value dimensions in which the system is so negative that there is no compensation for it. This means that the disadvantages of the system destroy all of its other advantages. A project can bring enormous negative ecological, social, and cultural impacts that no monetary gains can compensate.

4 Whole Systems and the Quality of Life

Systems theory suggests that the *quality of life* can be served by taking the view of whole systems. This requires considering all the relevant value dimensions, evaluating the performance of systems in adequate scales of measurement and using disqualification criteria for blocking trade-offs among non-substitutable values (Zsolnai 2008). In our ecologically fragile, socially disintegrating world the multidimensional decision making is a prerequisite for survival.

References

Kindler, J. and Papp, O. (1977), *Komplex rendszerek összemérése*. (Multi-criteria Evaluation of Complex Systems). Budapest, Műszaki Kiadó (in Hungarian).
Sen, A. (2009), *The Idea of Justice*. Harvard University Press, Cambridge, MA.

Tversky, A. (1972), "Elimination by aspects: A Theory of Choice" *Psychological Review*, Vol. 79, pp. 281–299.

Zsolnai, L. (2008), *Responsible Decision Making*. Transaction Publishers, New Brunswick & London.

CHAPTER 13

Redefining Economic Reason*

Despite *Martin Heidegger*'s warning, it's not modern technology but modern economizing that destroys the Being. With its exclusive focus on profit-making modern economizing endangers the integrity and diversity of natural ecosystems, autonomy, and culture of local communities, and the chances of future generations for a decent life.

This paper gives a critique of the profit principle and redefines economic rationality in a more holistic, substantive, and humanistic form.

1 Criticizing the Profit Principle

The devastating effects of profit-centered corporate business organizations are accurately described by American social critique David Korten. In his influential book *When Corporations Rule the World* he argues that today's global economy has become like a malignant cancer, advancing the colonization of the planet's living spaces for the benefit of powerful corporations and financial institutions. It has turned these once useful institutions into instruments of a market tyranny that is destroying livelihoods, displacing people, and feeding on life in an insatiable quest for money. It forces us all to act in ways destructive to ourselves, our families, our communities, and nature (Korten 1995).

*   First published: "Redefining Economic Reason" in H. Opdebeeck and L. Zsolnai (Eds) (2011), *Spiritual Humanism and Economic Wisdom*. Garant, Antwerp/ Apeldoom. pp. 187–200. Republished with the permission of Garant Publisher.

The economic and financial crisis started in 2008–2009 deepened our understanding of the problems of mainstream businesses which base their activities on unlimited greed and the 'enrich yourself' mentality.

There are two distinct but interrelated problems with the profit principle. One is how profit is the sole measure of rightness of economic activities and the other how profit is the main motivation of economic activities. We will see that profit is neither a necessary nor a sufficient criterion of economic reason.

1.1 Problems with Profit as the Measure

Profit is inadequate as the sole measure of the rightness of economic activities. Profit provides an incomplete and biased evaluation of economic activities. It reflects the values of the strongest stakeholders, favours preferences here and now, and presupposes the reducibility of all kind of values to monetary values.

The market as an evaluation mechanism has its inherent deficiencies. First of all, there are stakeholders that are simply not represented in determining market values. Natural beings and future generations do not have any opportunity to vote on the marketplace. Secondly, the preferences of human individuals count for rather less, that is, in proportion to their purchasing power; the interests of the poor and disadvantageous people are necessarily underrepresented in free market settings. Thirdly, the actual preferences of the market players are rather self-centered and myopic; that is, economic agents make their own decisions regarding short-term consequences only.

To use profit as the sole criterion of judging economic activities implies strong commensurability which means that there exists a common measure of the different values based on a cardinal scale of measurement. Mainstream economics suggests that values external to the market mechanism should be calculated by using shadow prices and other market-based evaluation techniques. In this way externalities can be 'internalized' and full cost pricing of activities can be developed.

Ecological economists demonstrated that the strong commensurability of values is not held in economics. The value of natural assets cannot adequately be expressed in monetary terms (McDaniel and Gowdy 2000). Similar arguments can be developed for important human and social values such as health and safety, ethics and aesthetics.

Profit can be used as an indicator of the financial viability of economic projects but not as an exclusive criterion of the rightness of economic activities. To judge the overall values of economic activities we should use a number of non-financial value-criteria in addition to financial ones.

The following scheme is an illustration of such a multimensional and holistic evaluation procedure.

The underlying idea of project evaluation is that a project is worthy of being undertaken if and only if the state of affairs with the project is better than the state of affairs without the project.

Let P be a project whose total monetary cost is p^*. Let Q be the original state of affairs, that is, the state of affairs without the project. Let Q^* be the new state of affairs, that is, the state of affairs with the project.

There are two alternative uses of the amount of money p^*. One alternative is to undertake project P by financing it with money p^*. The other alternative is not to undertake project P and use money p^* for financing other projects, e.g. investing in treasury bonds.

Let d (P) be the discounted cash flow that project P can produce for a given period of time. Let d (p^*) be the discounted total earnings of the amount of money p^* for the same period of time. So d (P) and d (p^*) represent two alternative uses of the same amount of money.

Let E(.) be a value function by which the state of affairs can be evaluated on ordinal scale from the ecological point of view.

$$\text{(I)} \quad E(Q) \; = \; \begin{cases} 1 & \text{if the state of affairs Q is beneficial for the nature;} \\ 0 & \text{if the state of affairs Q is neutral for the nature;} \\ -2 & \text{if the state of affairs Q is harmful for the nature.} \end{cases}$$

Let S(.) be value functions by which the state of affairs can be evaluated on ordinal scale from the social point of view. S(.) is also a Tversky-Kahneman type value function.

$$\text{(II)} \quad S(Q) \quad = \quad \begin{matrix} 1 \\ 0 \\ -2 \end{matrix} \quad \begin{matrix} \text{if the state of affairs Q is good for the society;} \\ \text{if the state of affairs Q is neutral for the society;} \\ \text{if the state of affairs Q is bad for the society.} \end{matrix}$$

Let M(.) be a monetary value function as follows:

$$\text{(III)} \quad M(P) \quad = \quad \begin{matrix} 1 \\ 0 \\ -2 \end{matrix} \quad \begin{matrix} \text{if the discounted cash flow d(P) is positive;} \\ \text{if the discounted cash flow d(P) is zero;} \\ \text{if the discounted cash flow d(P) is negative.} \end{matrix}$$

The following vector provides an overall evaluation of the original state of affairs:

(IV) $[E(Q), M(p^*), S(Q)]$

where $E(Q)$ and $S(Q)$ represent the environmental evaluation and the social evaluation of the original state of affairs and $M(p^*)$ represents the monetary evaluation of not undertaking the project.

An overall evaluation of the new state of affairs is provided by the following vector:

(V) $[E(Q^*), M(P), S(Q^*)]$

where $E(Q^*)$ and $S(Q^*)$ represent the environmental evaluation and social evaluation of the new state of affairs and $M(P)$ represents the monetary evaluation of the project itself.

The necessary and sufficient condition for undertaking the project is that the following preference relation is held:

(VI) $[E(Q^*), M(P), S(Q^*)] \quad \leftarrow \quad [E(Q), M(p^*), S(Q)]$

It means that the state of affairs with the project is better than the state of affairs without the project considering environmental, monetary, and social values simultaneously.

Social choice theory may help us to make decions in situation like (VI) where different components of the vectors are not necessarily comparable.

The multidimensional project evaluation outlined above can demonstrate that economic projects can be evaluated without accepting the strong commensurability assumption of mainstream economics. The crux of the matter is that we should extend the informational basis of analyses and braden the evaluative space beyond monetary values to include ecological and social values that cannot adequately be translated into monetary terms.

1.2 Problems with Profit as Motivation

Profit is dangerous as the main motivation for economic activities. It decreases intrinsic motivation of economic actors, which leads to decreasing quality. Also, it cultivates self-centered value orientation which results in socially insensitive and ethically irresponsible behavior.

Bruno Frey's 'crowding out' theory shows why profit motivation may be counter-productive. A monetary reward offered or expected tends to crowd out an agent's willingness to perform the task for its own sake (i.e. based on intrinsic motivation) if the agent's sense of recognition, fairness, or self-determination are thereby negatively affected. The crowding-out effect of pricing may also spill over into sectors where no pricing is applied (spillover effect) if the persons affected find it costly to dinstinguish their motivations according to sectors. Motivation crowding-out and spillover narrow the scope for successfully applying monetary rewards (Frey 1997).

The 'crowding out' mechanism has important consequences for the famous statement of Adam Smith that we can expect our bread not from the benevolence of the baker but from his self-love. Certainly, profit expectations provide strong incentives for the baker but producing truly healthy and beautiful bread requires something different: the priority of intrinsic commitment over monetary reward. The dangerous and unsustainable practice of modern agribusiness is a revealing illustration of the case (Zsolnai and Podmanicky 2010).

Personality psychologist Gian-Vittorio Caprara and his colleagues show emprically that cultivating greed leads to manipulation of others and oneself. They start with the observation that a division between thought and action takes place when people break the rules or get involved in illegal and unethical activities. What is most surprising in rule violation and misconduct is that people are not bothered by their conscience, do not fear any sanction, and do not feel obliged to make reparations (Caprara and Campana 2006).

World-renowned Stanford psychologist Albert Bandura discovered the mechanisms of moral disengagement, the psychosocial maneuvers by which moral self-sanctions become disengaged, leading to a variety of misbehaviors free of any moral concern. Self-sanctions can be disengaged by reconstructing the conduct, obscuring personal causal agency, misrepresenting or disregarding the injurious consequences of one's actions, and vilifying the recipients of maltreatment by blaming and devaluating them (Bandura 1990).

Caprara and his team developed a scale to assess civic moral disengagement (CMD). Their empirical findings suggest that the more people are concerned with self-enhancement goals, the more they are inclined to resort to mechanisms that permit them to disengage from the duties and obligations of civic life and to justify transgressions when their self-interest is at stake (Caprara and Campana 2006).

This result has another important consequence for the naive belief of Adam Smith and his followers in the always beneficial impact of the 'Invisible Hand' of the market. If economic agents become self-concerned then it is likely that – by employing moral disengagement mechanisms – their self-exonerative maneuvers will do harm to others.

In serving the common good we need agents who care about and pursue self and community interests.

1.3 Profit and Economic Reason

From the above analysis it follows that profit is neither a necessary nor a sufficient criterion of economic reason. An economic activity can be reasonable without satisfying the profit requirement. And inversely, the produced profit is not a guarantee that an economic activity is reasonable in a wider ecological and social context.

Economic reason should not be associated with economic rationality as defined and propagated by mainstream economics (Zsolnai 2008).

Today's theory of economic rationality is normatively inadequate and empirically misleading. James March rightly characterized it as the myth of rationality (March 2006). The reasonable action is an action that is based on right motivation, executed by fair processes, and leads to desirable outcomes (Sen 2004). We should try to redefine economic reason in accordance with the general criteria of reasonable action.

2 Redefining Economic Reason

Economic activities should pass the test of ecology, future generations, and society to be qualified for economic reason. This triple criteria require that economic activities should not destroy nature, violate the interests of future generations, or pose negative impacts on society. Economic actions can be claimed 'reasonable' only if they satisfy all of these criteria.

2.1 Ecology

From the perspective of nature ecological integrity is a central value. The notion of ecological integrity was introduced by American environmentalist Aldo Leopold in his classic *A Sand County Almanac*. He writes: "a thing is right when it tends to preserve the integrity, stability, and beauty of the biotic community. It is wrong when it tends otherwise." (Leopold 1948).

Economic activities might be evaluated against environmental indicators that operationalize the notion of ecological integrity.

Let A be an economic activity. Let $E1,...,Ej,...,En$ be environmental indicators ($n > 1$).

Ei(.) is an ecological value function defined as follows:

$$
(1)\ \ Ej(A) = \begin{cases} 1 & \text{if economic activity A is good regarding environmental indicator Ej;} \\ 0 & \text{if economic activity A is neutral regarding environmental indicator Ej;} \\ -2 & \text{if economic activity A is bad regarding environmental indicator Ej.} \end{cases}
$$

Ei(A) reflects the ecological value of economic activity A regarding environmental indicator Ej.

The following vector represents the ecological value of economic activity A regarding all environmental indicators E1,...,Ej,...,En.

(2) $E(A) = [E1(A),...,Ej(A),...,En(A)]$

To get an aggregate picture about the ecological value of the economic activity in question we should define weights that show the importance of environmental indicators. Let a1,...,aj,...,an be such importance weights.

It is required that

(3) $\sum aj = 1$

The aggregate ecological value of economic activity A can be calculated as follows:

(4) $E(A) = \sum aj\ Ej(A)$

E(A) shows the aggregate ecological value of economic activity A $(1 \geq E(A) \geq -2)$.

An economic activity is considered ecological if and only if its aggregate ecological value is positive. That is

(5) $E(A) \ > \ 0$

2.2 Future Generations

How can we evaluate economic activities from the perspective of future generations? We can never know much about the interests of future generations but freedom is a central value here.

Edith Brown Weiss argued that the freedom of future generations is insured by satisfying the following principles: (i) conservation of options; (ii) conservation of quality; and (iii) conservation of access (Brown Weiss 1989).

Considering principles (i),(ii), and (iii) future generations indicators can be created. Let $F1,...,Fj,...,Fn$ be such indicators against which economic activity system can be evaluated ($n > 1$).

Future generations value function $Fj(\ )$ is defined as follows:

$$(6)\quad Fj(A) = \begin{cases} 1 & \text{if economic activity A is good regarding future generation indicator Fj;} \\ 0 & \text{if economic activity A is neutral regarding future generations indicator Fj;} \\ -2 & \text{if economic activity A is bad regarding future generations indicator Fj.} \end{cases}$$

$Fj(A)$ reflects the future generations value of economic activity A regarding indicator Fj.

The following vector represents the future generations value of economic activity A regarding future generations indicators $F1,...,Fj,...,Fn$.

$$(7)\quad F(A) = [F1(A),...,Fj(A),...,Fn(A)]$$

To get an aggregate picture about the future generations value of economic activity A we should introduce weights that show the importance of indicators $F1,...,Fj,...,Fn$. Let $b1,...,bj,...,bn$ be such importance weights.

It is required that

$$(8)\quad \sum bj = 1$$

The aggregate future generations value of economic activity A can be calculated as follows:

(9) $\sum$ bj Fj(A)

F(A) shows the aggregate future generations value of economic activity A.
$(1 \geq F(A) \geq -2)$

An economic activity can be considered future respecting if its aggregate future generations value is positive. That is

(10) $F(A) > 0$

2.3 Society

Economic activities should be pro-social, that is should contribute to the development of people's capabilities.

Amartya Sen proposed to understand people's well-being in terms of capabilities. Capability is a reflection of the freedom of a person to achieve valuable functioning. Therefore capabilities can be interpreted as a substantive freedom that people enjoy (Sen 1992).

Let G1,...,Gj,...,Gn be capability indicators against which the economic activities can be evaluated $(j > 1)$.

Let Gj ( ) social value function be defined as follows:

(11) $Gj(A) = $
- 1   if economic activity A is good regarding capability indicator Gj;
- 0   if economic activity A is neutral regarding capability indicator Gj;
- -2   if economic activity A is bad regarding capability indicator Gj.

Gj(A) shows the social value of economic activity A regarding capability indicator Gj.

The following vector represents the social value of economic activity system A regarding all the capability indicators G1,...,Gj,...,Gn.

(12) $G(A) = [G1(A),...,Gj(A),...,Gn(A)]$

To get an aggregate picture about the social value of economic activity A we should introduce weights that show the importance of the capability indicators. Let $c1,...,cj,...,cn$ be such importance weights.
It is required that

(13) $\sum cj = 1$

The aggregate social value of economic activity A can be calculated as follows:

(14) $G(A) = \sum cj \, Gj(A)$

$G(A)$ shows the aggregate social value of the economic activity A $(1 \geq C(A) \geq -2)$.
An economic activity system is considered pro-social if its aggregate social value is positive. That is

(15) $G(A) > 0$

2.4 The Laws of Economizing

According to economic reason economic activities should be ecological, future respecting, and pro-social. For them (5), (10), and (15) should be simultaneously hold. That is

(16) $E(A) > 0, \quad F(A) > 0, \quad G(A) > 0$

From (16) we can derive some basic laws of economizing.

The First Law says that

(α) Economic activities should not harm nature or allow others to come
to harm.

The Second Law says that

(β) Economic activities must respect the freedom of future generations
except where such respect would conflict with the First Law.

The Third Law says that

(γ) Economic activities must serve the well-being of society as long as
such service does not conflict with the First or Second Law.

The main goal of economic activities should not be profit-making but
providing right livelihood for those who are involved. Economic reason
requires that this is achieved in ecological, future respecting, and pro-social
ways. Intrinsically motivated economic agents who balance their attention
and concerns across diverse value-dimensions are able to do this. Profit may
or may not follow but the richness of Being and the quality of life can be
attained. The Slow Food movement, ethical fashion, fair trade initiatives,
and ethical banking show the viability of true economic reason within the
present day 'rationally foolish' economic world.

References

Bandura, A. (1990), "Mechanisms of moral disengagement" in W. Reich (Ed.): *Origins
of Terrorism: Psychology, Ideologies, States of Mind*. Cambridge University Press,
Cambrige. pp. 45–103.

Brown Weiss, E. (1989), *In Fairness to Future Generations: International Law, Common Patrimony, and Intergeneration Equity*. The United Nations University, Tokyo & Transnational Publishers, Inc. Dobbs Ferry, New York.

Caprara, G-V. and Campana, C. (2006), "Moral Disengagement in the Exercise of Civic-ness" in L. Zsolnai (Ed): *Interdisciplinary Yearbook of Business Ethics*. Peter Lang, Oxford, pp. 85–96.

Frey, B. (1997), *Not Just for the Money*. Edward Elgar, UK.

Korten, D. (1995), *When Corporations Run the World*. Kumarian Press.

Leopold, A. (1948), *A Sand County Almanach*. Oxford University Press, Oxford.

McDaniel, C. and Gowdy, J. (2000), *Paradise for Sale: Regaining Sustainability – A Parable of Nature*. University of California Press.

March, J. (2006), "The Myth of Rationality" in L. Zsolnai (Ed): *Interdisciplinary Yearbook of Business Ethics*. Peter Lang, Oxford, pp. 17–29.

Sen, A. (1992), *Inequality Reexamined*. Russell Sage Foundation and Clarendon Press, New York and Oxford.

Sen, A. (2004), *Rationality and Freedom*. Harvard University Press, Cambridge, MA.

Zsolnai, L. (2008), *Responsible Decision Making*. Transaction Publishers, New Brunswick and London.

Zsolnai, L. and Podmanicky, L. (2010), "Community-Supported Agriculture" in Tencati, A. and Zsolnai, L. (Eds): *The Collaborative Enterprise: Creating Values for a Sustainable World*. Peter Lang, Oxford. pp. 137–152.

Index

Frontiers of Business Ethics

Series Editor
LASZLO ZSOLNAI
Business Ethics Center
Corvinus University of Budapest

This series is dedicated to alternative approaches that go beyond the literature of conventional business ethics and corporate social responsibility. It aims to promote a new ethical model for transforming business into humanistic, sustainable and peaceful forms. The series publishes monographs and edited volumes with fresh ideas and breakthrough conceptions relevant for scholars and practitioners alike.

VOLUME 1

Laszlo Zsolnai and Knut Johannessen Ims (eds):
Business within Limits: Deep Ecology and Buddhist Economics. 2005.
324 pages. ISBN 3-03910-703-8

VOLUME 2

Luigino Bruni and Stefano Zamagni:
Civil Economy: Efficiency, Equity, Public Happiness. 2007.
282 pages. ISBN 978-3-03910-896-1

VOLUME 3

Stig Ingebrigtsen and Ove Jakobsen:
Circulation Economics: Theory and Practice. 2007.
349 pages. ISBN 978-3-03911-089-6

VOLUME 4

Luk Bouckaert, Hendrik Opdebeeck and Laszlo Zsolnai (eds):
Frugality: Rebalancing Material and Spiritual Values in Economic Life.
2008. 322 pages. ISBN 978-3-03911-131-2

VOLUME 12

Laszlo Zsolnai:
  Beyond Self: Ethical and Spiritual Dimensions of Economics. 2014.
  203 pages. ISBN 978-3-0343-1772-6